Traveling EUROPE ON A BUDGET

An Insider's Guide to Finding Hidden Gems, Avoiding Tourist Traps
and Having the Vacation of Your Dreams on the Cheap

TONIA HOPE, *International Travel Guide*

PAGE STREET
PUBLISHING CO.

PAGE STREET
PUBLISHING CO.

First published in 2024 by
Page Street Publishing Co.
27 Congress Street, Suite 1511
Salem, MA 01970
www.pagestreetpublishing.com

Distributed by Macmillan, sales in Canada by The Canadian Manda Group.

28 27 26 25 24   1 2 3 4 5

ISBN-13: 978-1-64567-866-3
ISBN-10: 1-64567-866-0

Library of Congress Control Number: 2023936727

Edited by Franny Donington
Cover and book design by Elena Van Horn for Page Street Publishing Co.
Photography by Tonia Hope

Printed and bound in the United States of America

WANDERLUST

"a strong desire to travel"

For my family, friends and
supporters. May you all be
consumed by wanderlust.

Contents

INTRODUCTION

"To travel is to live." —Hans Christian Andersen

My "travel story" begins in the summer of 2015. I was embarking on my first solo trip across the world for an internship in China. I had never left the United Kingdom by myself before and had only traveled a handful of times in my life at that point. Of course, me being the fearless teenager that I was, I decided my first trip alone would be miles away from home to a country where I didn't speak the language. Yes, my mum was terrified (to this day I am still shocked she let me go). Looking back at it now, I was so brave. I felt nothing but curiosity and excitement from the moment I booked my flight to the first step I took on Shanghai soil. This trip completely opened my eyes to the joy that can be experienced when traveling. The adrenaline of navigating a new city, meeting new people, trying unique activities, making mistakes and then making more mistakes. I instantly fell in love with travel. There is some truth to the saying that we fear more things when we age, because the idea of doing that now gives me knots in my stomach. Following this monumental trip, I just kept going and haven't stopped since.

Next, I had my sights set on exploring slightly closer to home, Europe. The continent of Europe, with its historical significance, breathtaking scenery and amazing wine is an irresistible allure for everyone. The continent is so diverse, with each country offering something unique and special to all who visit. I'm fortunate enough to have Europe on my doorstep, which means I am a frequent visitor. Don't tell my accountant this, but if I had the time, I would explore a different country every month of the year. It's a region I love and could never get tired of visiting. From the bustling streets of London to the romantic allure of Paris, the lucky charm of Dublin to the exotic mystique of Budapest, the ancient ruins of Rome to the canals of Amsterdam (I could pretty much go on for months), the European experience is an intricate mosaic of destinations.

After a few years of travel, I finally gained the confidence to start sharing my adventures online in the hopes that others would be encouraged to go and experience it for themselves. Hence, the Tonia Hope brand was born. By sharing my travels online, I have been able to connect with an amazing community worldwide, which has been so helpful and rewarding over the years. I have been given amazing recommendations and advice on countless trips. Personally, I love a good recommendation. Not only does it save me heaps of time researching, reading reviews

and working out logistics, but it also often means I am able to encounter things I otherwise would have missed.

A common misconception is that travel must be expensive and it's only for those with access to "Daddy's money" or a six-figure tech salary, but it can be so much more affordable than you think. Speaking from experience, my travel hobby did not start with either of these things. You may be thinking, *Can you really visit Europe on a budget?* The answer is a resounding "Yes!" There are so many ways to cut costs without compromising an epic trip. This book aims to not only inspire you to travel across Europe, but more importantly, give you practical advice, tips and the knowledge to do so.

Furthermore, don't think that just because this is a budget travel guide that we will only be covering the cheapest of hostels. I still like to have a nice, somewhat luxurious feel to my travel and accommodations, so we will be talking about how to marry the two for the best price. I have aimed to thread my "bougie on a budget" mentality throughout the locations and chapters.

As we delve in to ten places you need to visit in Europe, remember that the heart of travel isn't just in lavish hotels or 5-star meals, but in the connections and memories you create along the way. Consider me a big sister guiding you through a world of affordable European adventures that will reshape the way you perceive travel. Let's go . . .

SO, YOU WANT TO TRAVEL?

In the quiet corners of our minds, there often lingers a yearning for exploration, a thirst to break free from the ordinary and embark on a journey into the unknown and unfamiliar.

Europe, with its rich history, diverse cultures and stunning landscapes, stands as a playground for adventurers seeking to quench that thirst. Eventually, you find yourself at a crossroads, contemplating the idea of traveling around Europe. However, you may not be sure whether it's possible to make this trip work on a budget (this has been me on many occasions).

No idea where to start with planning? This chapter will answer all your questions and guide you through the initial steps of turning your travel dreams into a tangible reality.

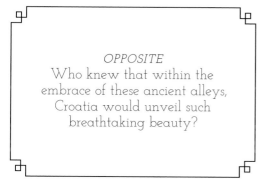

OPPOSITE
Who knew that within the embrace of these ancient alleys, Croatia would unveil such breathtaking beauty?

DREAM BIG

All great things that have ever been achieved began with an idea, and so does your budget-friendly European escapade. Just imagine yourself waking up one morning to a luscious view of the Eiffel Tower, or running to catch a red bus in London or relaxing in a remote thermal pool in Iceland. Sounds like an incredible dream, right? Just allow yourself to imagine the sight of all the iconic landmarks before you, the taste of tantalizing cuisines touching your tongue and all the stories you'll have to share on social media or, even better, through postcards you send home from each location you visit. Let this fuel your determination to make traveling to Europe a reality, regardless of any budget worries.

SET YOUR GOALS

The first thing you should do when planning an epic bucket list trip is define your goals for the trip. Is your primary goal to immerse yourself in new cultures? Hiking adventures? Food tourism? Or just a mix of everything? I sit in the camp of going for a mix of everything. I have literally been on trips where I hiked one day, spent the entire next day at a spa and followed it all up with a street food tour. Being able to decide what draws you to traverse Europe will make shaping your itinerary and travel route easier. Also, knowing what's most important to you will help guide decisions on where to prioritize allocating your budget. Whether you are a nature lover, a spa girlie or love touring art museums, I'll cover a range of affordable experiences for every type of travel you are looking for.

RESEARCH

Ever heard of the phrase "the more you know"? If you were only going to do one thing before embarking on a trip, it should be doing thorough research. Learn about the most budget-friendly times of year to travel, the best local transportation options, affordable accommodations, whether that's a hostel or a guesthouse and hidden gems that may not be as well known but offer unforgettable experiences. Fortunately, each of these topics is covered in the guides within this book. However, I'm sure I didn't even need to mention this at all to you super savvy readers, as you've already purchased this book!

Of course, there is always room for extra knowledge, especially for those of you reading this book in 20 years from the date it was published (I definitely have high hopes). When it comes to the world of travel, things can change quite rapidly, especially in the age of technology. Who knows, in a few years scientists may perfect teleportation, which would render many transportation options obsolete. This is specifically important when it comes to government regulations. I've seen this firsthand, as the UK left the European Union in a flash. This book will still be super helpful, because I've designed it to be as timeless as possible.

On the other hand, sometimes rules and regulations change over time, so it's still worth doing some additional research. For example, when I visited Krka National Park in October 2019, I was able to swim in the waterfall; however, by January 2020 swimming in the waterfall was banned.

Speaking of changes: From mid-2025, US travelers between 18 and 70 years old will need to fill out an **ETIAS visa-waiver form** prior to visiting Europe and pay a €7 (just under $8 approximately) entry fee to travel to European countries within the Schengen Area. It's a relatively quick form and approval shouldn't take much time, but it's important to apply with ample time and to factor this in when making budget decisions, as every little bit helps!

DECIDING YOUR BUDGET

A budget is more than just a few numbers; it's a tool that empowers you to make the most of your resources. My recommendation is that you start by looking at your bank statements and spending habits to assess how much you can comfortably allocate to your travel adventure. Don't forget, it's always great to estimate it to be more than you've calculated everything will cost. A good budget has some room for flexibility; for example, toward the end of the trip you may be sick of shared hostel dorms and want a night in a 5-star hotel. In addition, you never know when an emergency may occur. The worst case is you return home with spare money and have a head start budget-wise for your next adventure.

Everyone will have their own way of making a budget, but I like to work off my monthly salary. I take the amount paid into my account for one month and split it using the 50/30/20 rule. For me personally, that looks like 50 percent toward my travel budget, 30 percent toward bills and daily expenses and 20 percent toward long-term investments and savings. Then, I put the 50 percent toward the first elements of planning a trip: flights and accommodations. From there, I do the same with my next month's pay, and take half to put toward spending on activities and food while I am away.

All the country guides included in this book will give you a great indication of how much you'll be spending in each location. Make sure you are weighting your budget according to what you outlined as your goals. Don't be daunted by how much the numbers add up; in the next chapter, "Financing Your Dream," (page 13) we will delve more in to how to raise additional funds if necessary or even travel for FREE.

CRAFTING YOUR ITINERARY

Now let's take some action behind these goals, because a goal without a plan is just a wish, and we are the kind of people who make things happen! As you begin to draft your itinerary, make sure you strike a balance between iconic tourist hot spots, must-see attractions and off-the-beaten-path experiences. I usually draft everything in the Notes app on my iPhone, so it can be easily edited; however, a few of my friends prefer to have things written down on paper in a notebook. I often hear people talk about how everyone goes to the same places, and they don't like to be tourists but "travelers," but the truth is most people are visiting as tourists. There's no point visiting London and then only going to the suburbs to see people's houses. There is a reason many tourist hot spots are popular; for instance, I could never imagine visiting Rome without visiting the Colosseum, especially on a first visit. Moral of the story: Don't be too hard on yourself.

My number one rule for visiting Europe is to visit multiple countries in one trip, otherwise known as "country coupling." It's so easy to get between different countries inexpensively. Make the best use of budget airlines, such as **Ryanair** and **Wizz Air**. Alternatively, the inter-country train network is impeccable and easy to use. For example, the journey from central London to central Paris is two hours by the **Eurostar** train network, and if you book far enough in advance, the prices are very affordable. **Eurail** and **Interrail** offer very affordable train ticket passes for across Europe, which could really reduce your inter-country travel costs. I have used the train networks to travel from England to France, Germany, the Netherlands, Switzerland, Italy and more.

ADAPTING AND EMBRACING

Travel is a dynamic journey; flexibility is your friend! I can't even count the number of times things have strayed from the plan on my trips. I have missed flights, lost items, had timelines changed, had trains canceled, booked accommodations that do not exist, overspent majorly, been harassed and more. It's fair to say things haven't always gone perfectly. However, one thing all great travelers have in common is being able to adapt in unexpected circumstances. Hopefully your travels aren't as dramatic as mine, but being open to changing which island you explore in Greece or finding alternative travel methods when there's bad weather will go a long way. Be open to seizing opportunities that might not be part of a meticulously planned itinerary. These often make for the best stories and experiences.

ADVENTURE AWAITS

I'm sure all the above has really gotten your imaginative brain juices flowing, but this was just a taster. Wait until you hear more about all the unbelievable things Europe has in store for you. Let's get into how you're going to afford it.

FINANCING YOUR DREAM

The big question when it comes to travel is how people afford to go, especially when it comes to pricier areas of the world, like Europe. There is a running joke on social media that as soon as June hits, it's time for everyone to start wondering how everyone is able to afford their trips to Europe. On my social media channels, I am asked at least once a day how I afford to travel. We will go over that in great detail in this book, but here are a range of suggestions on how to begin financing your travel, with some examples of suggestions I have benefited from.

PRIME YOUR LIFE AND BRAIN FOR SAVING

It may seem obvious, but it's worth pointing out that if you want to travel the world, you need to be thinking frugally about your everyday spending.

When I finished university, I decided to move back home. The major reason for doing this was because it was the most cost-effective decision for me, as I wanted to continue prioritizing travel in my life, even though I had gotten my first "big girl" job days before my graduation ceremony. I knew moving back to my family home would put me in the best position financially. Guess where I still live now?!

Yes, I still live at home, and over the last few years I have saved thousands on rent and expenses (I say "saved" but a fair amount was in fact spent on travel). I am aware this may not be a feasible option for everyone, but if it is something available to you, I'd strongly consider it. An alternative could be getting a roommate or renting out a spare room if you have one available.

You'd be shocked how many people have direct debits for things they rarely make use of. For example, there is no reason to have a gym membership if you only visit occasionally or having a beauty subscription box service when it would be more cost-effective to buy the items when you need them. You could live without these things for a few months while you're preparing for your trip. No judgments from me of course, as I've had my fair share of enjoyment with subscription services, but it's time to have an honest conversation with yourself.

Alternatively, you could investigate sharing some subscriptions with a friend to reduce the costs. For instance, if you live in the same house with a friend, you could share an Amazon Prime delivery service. Unfortunately, sharing Netflix passwords and a few other streaming platforms are now a thing of the past due to recent changes.

If you're looking for a flexible way to increase your income, you can use your existing skills and start a side hustle from home. Great at Excel? Good with money management? Got a knack for social media? Do you speak another language? Have a degree in teaching primary school children? Signing up to **Fiverr** is a good way to monetize your skills around your current schedule. When I first started my social media pages, it was just a fun hobby and I had no idea it would turn into something I could be paid for. I was just excited to be able to create, network with people and constantly talk about travel with people who would never get sick of it. Next thing I knew, I was making enough to fund all my travels. Don't have a platform? If you're a creative, consider delving in to the world of **User-generated content**, where brands pay creators to make content for their channels.

Lifestyle inflation is when the amount you spend increases the more your income increases (this does not include increased spending due to inflation). To illustrate, say you make homemade lunch for work every day, get a promotion and then decide to now buy lunch every day instead. The extra income that could have been directed to reaching your travel savings goals is gone. The more you monitor and track your spending, the easier it is to see small changes in your finances.

CREATE A SPECIFIC BANK ACCOUNT FOR TRAVEL

Have a separate bank account dedicated to just your travel savings. This will minimize temptations to dip in to the fund for other expenses, and you can monitor your progress easily. Some accounts even allow you to set a "savings goal" for the account. This should be a High Yield Savings Account (HYSA), which just means the bank pays you a good interest rate on the money you have saved with them. So, each month your money remains in the bank, the bank will add an extra few dollars as a reward for keeping your money there. Current great options are a **SoFi Bank** savings account (US) and **Monzo Bank** (UK). I use this method to organize my entire life, and it does wonders.

Also, when you've decided how frequently you'd like to be putting money aside for your European escapades, set up an automatic payment system. For example, each payday, money will automatically be transferred to your savings account, so you don't have to worry about forgetting.

LEAN IN TO YOUR GLOBAL NETWORK

Accommodation can be one of the most expensive aspects of traveling, but using the people you know could significantly help you reduce these costs or eliminate them. Something I've always done is use my global network (and even sometimes my friends' and family's networks). For example, I've stayed at the homes of distant cousins and international friends when I've been visiting a city. Don't have any friends or family abroad? No matter, there are other ways to access this network. Many Facebook groups that focus on travel offer something similar. One of my favorites is the **Host A Sister** Facebook community, where a group of lovely women around the world make offers and requests for accommodation in cities across Europe (and the world). Other great options are signing up for **Couch-Surfing**, where you can stay on someone's couch or in their spare room for a few bucks or for free. If you're lucky, you might even get someone who will cook you breakfast, as I did in Iceland. If you'd prefer to have somewhere to yourself, you should consider international house-sitting or pet-sitting. Some useful sites for looking for available options are **Trusted Housesitters**, **Nomador**, **HouseCarers** and **MindMyHouse**.

RESEARCH GRANTS AND SCHOLARSHIPS

When I initially started traveling, I was an 18-year-old student in my first year of university. Students are notoriously known for having tight budgets and little disposable income. Knowing my circumstances, I decided to get creative and discovered the blessing that is grants and scholarships. One day I was scouring my university student resources and came across an "International Experience Bursary,"

which was essentially free money to undertake a trip abroad. Similarly, on another occasion I was doing some random Google searches on "how to get funding for travel" and I came across a fully funded immersive program being offered by the British Council for a trip to India. Unexpectedly, I applied to both and managed to be chosen for both!

After these trips, I had officially caught the travel bug and knew this wouldn't be the end. Throughout my time at university, I continued to apply for every travel opportunity I saw that had free funding, which landed me a funded year abroad in Canada, among other opportunities.

So, why am I telling you this? Long story short, I have seen countless opportunities available for Europe. Now, you may be thinking, *Well, Tonia, I am not a student anymore* or *I didn't go to college*, so this doesn't apply to you, but you would be wrong. You'd be shocked to know that scholarships and travel grants aren't just for young people or students. There are so many opportunities available for people at all stages of life. A great place to begin your search is **Packs Light** Paid Travel Opportunity Board. Gabby Beckford at Packs Light is an amazing content creator who collates hundreds of paid travel opportunities that cater to people of all ages.

VOLUNTEER AND WORK EXCHANGE

Many hostels, hotels and companies offer volunteer packages in exchange for room and board. You can use websites such as **Workaway**, **HelpX**, **Worldpackers**, **Volunteer Forever** and **Working Traveller** to find specific opportunities and programs. There is a wide variety of options available, such as running social events, handling social media accounts, housekeeping, administration and much more.

SELL UNWANTED CLOTHES AND ITEMS

Consider decluttering your wardrobe or living space by selling items you no longer need or use. This benefits you not only through giving you extra income for your travel fund, but it also declutters your life and space. A few years ago, I had a complete room makeover and truly realized how much stuff I essentially didn't remember owning. I soon became obsessed with **eBay** and rehoming all my unwanted items for a little extra income to pay for the renovations, and it was a complete success. Other great sites and apps for selling clothes and unwanted goods are **Vinted**, **Depop** and **Facebook Marketplace**.

USE CARD POINTS AND AIRLINE LOYALTY PROGRAMS

Becoming a member of a travel loyalty program is a must for anyone who loves to travel. You can collect points through credit cards, many of which offer huge sign-up bonuses. The main providers are **Chase Bank** and **American Express**. Points can be used on things like flights, accommodation, rental cars, hotels, travel insurance, transfers and other travel expenses. Don't forget to ensure you are using your credit card responsibly.

In addition, many airlines have specific credit cards available that reward brand loyalty with substantial points systems. Some popular brands are **JetBlue®** (Barclays), **Delta Air Lines®** (American Express), **American Airlines®** (Mastercard) and **United Airlines®** (CHASE).

However, if you aren't a fan of credit cards, you can still collect points. **British Airways Executive Club** allows members to collect points on their app through everyday shopping purchases. All you need to do is sign up, link a bank card and it'll automatically apply points to eligible purchases. Points earned can be used on British Airways products but can also be used on products offered by all airlines included in the oneworld Alliance: Alaska Airlines®, American Airlines, Cathay Pacific, Finnair, Iberia, Japan Airlines, Malaysia Airlines, Qantas, Qatar Airways, Royal Air Maroc, Royal Jordanian and SriLankan Airlines. I recently took a flight to Edinburgh using my Avios points and ended up saving $120.

MY TOP 10 SAVING TIPS

Over the years, I have traveled on every budget imaginable, which means that along the way I have picked up many tricks, so here are my top 10 savings tips for traveling around Europe. These range from being useful during the booking process to while you are gallivanting around the continent. These are in no particular order; I consistently use each one of these to save money.

1. USE PRICE COMPARISON WEBSITES

Skyscanner and **Google Flights** are a godsend. Both sites have great features to ensure you are able to make informed budget decisions when booking flights. Features to note are Skyscanner's "savings generator" to see when the most affordable time to book is for your chosen destination in Europe. In addition, the "everywhere" feature is also a great one for choosing which location to visit next. If you opt to visit multiple countries in Europe, it shows the cheapest destination to fly from your chosen airport. Google Flights has a great flight tracker tool, so you can set up alerts for price drops. Other great sites are **Kiwi.com**, **Opodo**, **Expedia** and **KAYAK®**. You can save significant amounts by changing your flights by even one day.

2. LOOK OUT FOR ERROR FARES

Error fares are the result of airlines accidentally putting the wrong price for a ticket listing on their website, which means flight prices are much lower than they typically would be. It often occurs because the fuel costs per passenger is missing, which is usually the bulk of the cost. These prices tend to only last a few hours on the sites before the error is fixed, so if you purchase your ticket before then, the price you purchased at is likely to be honored, resulting is greatly discounted tickets. You'd be shocked to know how often this happens! I have grabbed several great bargains over the years. An easy way of finding these is signing up to **Jack's Flight Club**, **HolidayPirates**, **Going™** and **Secret Flying**. They often send out emails when they spot a deal and let you know how long those prices will last on the site. Of course, this is a riskier trick, as the airline could cancel your ticket if you've booked months in advance. I would advise booking accommodation, activities and so on closer to the time of departure to be certain.

3. DON'T TRAVEL WITH ROLLING LUGGAGE

This will help you not only pack light and avoid spending extra on heavy bags, but Europe does not bode well for rolling luggage. Many streets are cobblestone and staircases are narrow, depending on where you decide to visit (I'm looking at you, Portugal), and the pavement can be very uneven and hilly. Additionally, many airlines only include a free "personal item" as luggage, so adding hand luggage or checked luggage means costly add-ons. Instead, travel light with a backpack and use **vacuum packing bags** to maximize the space.

4. NEVER EXCHANGE MONEY AT THE AIRPORT

I know, it seems like a super convenient way to change your money and it's tempting, but if you're on a budget this is a big no-no. These merchants offer exchange rates that are much less favorable than those your home bank offers. So, skip the airport kiosks and head to a local bank ATM for the best rates. Depending on where you are traveling, you may not need cash at all.

5. ALWAYS OPT TO PAY IN LOCAL CURRENCY INSTEAD OF YOUR HOME CURRENCY

Like Tip 4, paying in your home currency will mean you aren't getting the best exchange rate, so you are losing money when you don't have to. For example, when paying by card, many card readers will ask whether you would prefer to pay in the local currency (most likely euros) or US dollars. When given the option, always choose to pay in the local currency. I'm looking at you, US travelers: It's tempting to use US dollars, but it'll cost you!

6. USE ELIGIBLE DISCOUNTS

Many places offer concession discounts for a variety of demographics. If you have a student, OAP or Armed Forces ID, then you could benefit from an up to 30 percent discount on rail, admissions tickets to attractions, museums, tours and so much more. Always remember to check when paying whether you're eligible for any discounts. Don't have any of these? Try to visit a **Tourist Information Point**. Besides providing free information and advice, tourist offices in Europe often have coupon and voucher booklets that include discounts for sights, tours, restaurants, museums and more.

7. GET TO KNOW YOUR AIRBNB HOSTS

A handy tip I learned recently is to keep the Airbnb host details from good stays I've had in their property. Many owners have multiple properties across the country as well as the continent. When I am traveling to another area of the country and need accommodation, I will message them and see whether they have any rental properties there. Usually, they would much rather book someone they are familiar with and know is a good guest to stay there. This is also a good segue to ask for a discount on this stay if you pay in cash. This removes money being taken for platform fees and benefits both parties. Similarly, this works for guest houses and some smaller hotel chains.

8. GET TRAVEL INSURANCE

Travel insurance is a crucial safety net. The savings from purchasing this won't be immediate but will pay off in the long run. Since the pandemic, travel numbers have been at an all-time high. This is great news for the public; however, this has resulted in an increased likelihood of things potentially going wrong. Suitcases going missing, overbooked flights, trip interruptions and medical emergencies are all covered. When choosing a policy, make sure you read the terms and conditions, as different packages offer a different level of coverage. Traveling in Europe should be about enjoyment, and with travel insurance you will have peace of mind. I use **SafetyWing** for my extensive travels. I recommend seeing what works for you on travel insurance comparison websites like **Comparethemarket**, **TravelSupermarket**, **Skyscanner**, **InsureMyTrip** or **Squaremouth**.

9. PACK A REFILLABLE WATER BOTTLE

Carrying a refillable water bottle while you travel has more benefits than just helping you stay hydrated. Purchasing bottled water numerous times a day can end up costing a small fortune, especially in tourist areas where prices may be inflated. Using a refillable water bottle means you can save money by refilling from tap sources. In Rome, there are water fountains dotted all around the city with fresh water. It was super fun running around the city looking for them. Furthermore, using a refillable water bottle is much better for the environment than purchasing plastic bottles. Less cost to you and less cost to the planet.

10. CHOOSE THE RIGHT ROAMING PLAN

International roaming charges are pretty steep; therefore, you need to make sure you are choosing the right roaming plan, whether this is an add-on to your existing regular contract or you decide to opt for an eSIM. My current phone contract is with O2, and I have a monthly contract that includes roaming charges. This means I can use my inclusive allowances (e.g., 30 GB of data) like I do at home in the UK. Most major US phone networks offer this, including **T-Mobile®**, **Google Fi Wireless**, **AT&T®** and **Sprint**. Alternatively, an eSIM is a programmable small chip that is built into most modern smartphones during manufacturing. Long story short, this allows for a connection to a phone provider without inserting an actual physical sim card. Essentially, you will be buying a short-term phone contract that works abroad. Some great eSIM providers are **Airalo**, **Nomad**, **Simify** and **Drimsim**. Something to be aware of is these providers only offer data, as opposed to calls or text packages.

London
IT'S CALLING, YOU SHOULD ANSWER!

Of course, I must kick off this book by paying homage to my home city, London. I have lived in London my entire life and have fallen in love with the city repeatedly over the years. And before you ask, no I haven't met any of the royal family. However, funnily enough my sisters and mom met Queen Elizabeth II at a borough celebration engagement a few years ago. Unfortunately, I was abroad and missed it . . . sigh! There are so many things I love about London: the diversity of people, the delicious international cuisines, the endless unique activities to keep me occupied and the epic blend of historical traditions coupled with bustling modern culture. All of these make London an interesting and exciting destination to visit. Anyone who says the city is overrated probably hasn't done it right, but as your residential insider guiding you, that won't be you. However, London may just be one of the most expensive cities in Europe to visit, but there will be no gatekeeping on my watch. This chapter will contain everything you need to know about visiting London on a budget.

CITY PROFILE

Currency, Bank Cards & ATMs: The Great British Pound (GBP) is the currency used throughout England. The UK is one of the only countries in geographical Europe that does not use the euro. I once had a friend visit me in the UK from the United States who had converted US dollars into euros for her trip. It's safe to say I will never be letting her live it down.

London is very much a cashless society, to the extent that many places do not accept cash. Some people even predict cash could go extinct within the city in the near future. You can use a bank card (Mastercard, Visa and American Express are all accepted) to pay for almost everything around the city. I rarely ever find myself withdrawing cash for many things in my everyday life, except for takeaways from smaller local restaurants. Fortunately, for you, this means you can use your existing bank cards to spend here.

If for some reason you do need cash, you'll be pleased to know you can pretty much find an ATM on every street corner in London. To save money, avoid ATMs that have a charge, as there are plenty of ATMs available to use free of charge around the city. Download the **AroundMe** app. The app identifies your GPS position and will let you know where the nearest ATM, bank, bar, gas station, hospital, accommodation, cinema, supermarket, restaurant and taxi are. Pretty neat right?

Climate: Not sure if you've heard, but London has a reputation for being gray, unfortunately. However, that isn't technically true. London mostly has a mild and pleasant climate year round, which can be variable at different points during the year. The country's hottest months are June to August; however, this also means that it is peak season for tourism. You should consider visiting in spring (March to May) for more favorable prices. Also, spring is a popular time to visit as the weather begins to warm up and flowers begin to bloom. You'll be treated to gorgeous cherry blossoms in Greenwich Park, the Regent's Park and St. James's Park.

OPPOSITE
The iconic London Eye on a crisp, brisk England afternoon.

Furthermore, Christmas in London is truly something very special, so if you are happy to brave the cold it is a great time to visit. The festive atmosphere means Christmas markets, ice rinks, decorations and merriment. One of my favorite things about the winter season in London are the light displays on Oxford Street (it's a whole big thing here!).

 Safety: London has consistently been ranked one of the safest cities in the world. Most trips here are trouble free, and I genuinely recommend it as a great place for first-time solo travelers and veteran travelers alike. You will find it comforting that as a local, I have never felt unsafe navigating the city at any time, even at night. Moreover, I have many friends in the travel community who have visited, and each trip has been trouble-free. However, please remember safety precautions are necessary wherever you visit in the world and every city has its flaws. Stay aware of your surroundings, plan your routes and keep valuables concealed while on public transport. London is very welcoming, so feel free to enjoy the culture, explore attractions and visit hidden gems in peace.

 Language: English is the most widely spoken language by far in London, and it is the official language of the UK. However, London has an amazing multicultural population, which means there is a rich diversity of languages spoken by different communities. Did you know the second most spoken language in London is Bengali? So interesting, right?

VISITING ON A BUDGET

HOTEL & STAYS

Regardless of where you stay, getting around London is super easy (it's much smaller than you'd think), so if you're on a budget and choosing the more affordable option, you'll still have a great experience immersed in it all. Here are my recommendations:

Low budget: Generator London ($–$$), located in King's Cross. This modern, stylish hostel offers a range of great amenities, including various events for socializing, lounge areas and a bar. Also nearby is **Clink78 Hostel ($–$$)**. This unique hostel is situated in a former courthouse and offers a great mix of private and shared dormitories to suit your budget. **St. Christopher's Inn ($–$$)** has locations near London Bridge, as well as other central locations across London. My favorite branch, **St. Christopher's Inn Greenwich ($)**, is just outside of Greenwich station. You'll be met with friendly staff and great amenities, such as an outdoor terrace. It's perfect for the summer and at a great price point. In addition, **Astor Hyde Park Hostel ($–$$)** is super central and located next to the famous Hyde Park. Another option is **Wombat's City Hostel London ($–$$)**, located a short walk away from the bustling creative hub that is Shoreditch.

Low to mid-budget: Don't forget to check out the prices at **Travelodge ($–$$)**, **Premier Inn ($–$$)** and **Ibis Hotels ($–$$)** for your dates. These budget chain hotel options offer very comfortable rooms for affordable prices, sometimes identical to hostel prices. These hotels are within a close distance to the city center, so it is easy to travel in.

Mid-budget: The Resident Covent Garden ($$–$$$$) is a luscious boutique hotel that offers stylish rooms in the heart of Covent Garden. Perfect for a good night's sleep after a late show at the theater. Furthermore, both **The Culpeper ($$)** and **The Hoxton ($$–$$$)** are lovely boutique hotel options that I have enjoyed.

Student accommodation: University Rooms offer no-frills affordable accommodation. During the summer, most students move out of their university halls, and these are left vacant until classes resume in the fall. If you check the website for around September, you can find great rooms with a central location for the same price as most shared room hostels. They have bed and breakfasts or self-catering budget accommodations scattered across 120 cities worldwide.

OPPOSITE
You'll love the variety of modern
and rustic hostel styles dotted
throughout the city!

TRANSPORTATION

Getting there: Let's start with getting from the airport into the city. I know you may be tempted, but do not, I repeat DO NOT get the Express train from the airport if you are on a budget. If you are flying into Heathrow airport, the Piccadilly line takes you straight into London for a fraction of the price. If your budget is super tight, I recommend great coach options, such as the **National Express** bus.

Next, the famous **Visitor Oyster card**. This is a smart card that offers discounted fares on the London transport network system, and it is by far the most cost-effective way of getting around the city. As a bonus, some attractions in London offer discounts if you show your Oyster card when paying for entry. Check the official websites of attractions you plan to visit for any available deals. Some of my favorites include 20 percent off your bill at **Southbank Vapianos** Monday to Friday and 15 percent off your entire in-store purchase at **M&M World** in Leicester Square.

As previously mentioned, in London we're obsessed with contactless payments! So, of course you can also use contactless payment methods, which offer the same benefits as using an Oyster card. This includes a daily and weekly cap on how much you can spend. Once you reach the daily cap, any additional travel you do that day is essentially "free."

Traveling outside off-peak times will also ease the cost of traveling around London. Peak times are the busiest times of day that people (mostly commuters) are using the transport network, which means Transport for London charges higher usage fees at this time. This is particularly relevant for traveling by the London Underground. Peak times run from 6:30 to 9:30 a.m. and 4:00 to 7:00 p.m. Off-peak fares are generally lower, especially for traveling around Zone 1, which is where the majority of the most popular tourist attractions are.

Buses: Buses offer a flat rate fare for rides, so if you do need to travel during peak times, explore the possibility of taking a bus route. Unfortunately, this may mean more time in traffic. This would be the perfect time for me to introduce you to the hopper fare. The hopper fare means that you can take multiple buses within one hour at no extra charge. In addition, no matter how many buses or trams you take in a day, it will never cost you more than £5.25 total, thanks to the daily cap again. Just make sure you use the same payment method and card for every journey. To note, London buses do not accept cash payments.

Walking: London is a very walkable city, and major attractions are located within walking distance of each other. I have frequently walked from Westminster to the Soho area to meet friends and it's such a lovely way to get around. On my route, I pass the Houses of Parliament, Trafalgar Square and more. Additionally, areas like Covent Garden, Leicester Square and Oxford Street can all be explored without paying for transport in between.

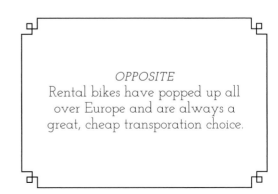

OPPOSITE
Rental bikes have popped up all over Europe and are always a great, cheap transporation choice.

Biking: Additionally, you can easily rent a bike through the **Santander Cycles Scheme**, commonly referred to as "Boris Bikes," for short trips around the city. This costs around $2 (£1.65) for every 30 minutes of riding.

Cabs: Last, if you need a cab to get from points A to B quickly, do not use a black cab if you're on a tight budget. Order a car through the **Uber**, **Bolt** or **FreeNow** apps. All work around the city and cost a fraction of the price of a black cab.

FOOD & DRINK

If there is one thing that London does right, it is food and drink. Whether you're desperate to try a traditional British meal of fish and chips or grab a quick bubble tea at Leicester Square, there is something for every palate. London has a very vibrant food scene that reflects its multicultural population and rich culinary traditions. Cheap eats are pretty much everywhere in London. Not only are they well priced, but the food is also delicious.

"Food is our common ground, a universal experience."
- James Beard

Street food: Take advantage of street food markets. London has a variety of street food markets where you can find delicious and affordable options for every meal. **Camden Market** and **Borough Market** are both ones I highly recommend; however, they do get very busy. In Camden Market, I am absolutely obsessed with **Meat Head Mexican** and their birria tacos. Each taco is so juicy and delicious. I never hesitate to grab one whenever I am in the area. Also, **Asador** serves up absolute mouthwatering Argentinean rib-eye steaks. Moving on to Borough Market, **JUMA Kitchen** is an absolute MUST TRY. Their cuisine celebrates the best of Iraqi cuisine, and I am obsessed with everything on the menu. You can grab any of these foods for a few pounds and be kept full for the next few hours. The portions are reasonable and the atmosphere is buzzing. Other affordable market options include **Brick Lane Market**, **Maltby Street Market** and **Broadway Market**, which sell a variety of cheap eats to grab on the go.

Supermarkets: Popular supermarket chains like **Tesco**, **Sainsbury's** and **Marks & Spencer** all have meal deal offers whereby you can grab a sandwich, snack and a drink for a fixed price. This is a great option for keeping costs low during lunch, or any meal really. It's quick, convenient and very affordable. **Greggs** is another great option for a grab-and-go lunch. Here you can get sausage rolls, bakes, pastries and much more.

Pubs: Some pubs offer great affordable meal options that include traditional British dishes like pies and mash commonly known as pub grub. Look out for pub grub deals. Here are a few pubs in central London that are known for offering great pub grub deals. **Wetherspoons** is a British staple, especially at the airport before a flight. It's known for budget-friendly prices and daily deals. They have multiple locations across London and in my opinion, this is a local's spot. Other options include **The Chandos** near Trafalgar Square, **The Porterhouse**, **Lamb & Flag** and **Lyceum Tavern** in Covent Garden and **The Crown Tavern**. Make sure you keep an eye out for chalkboard specials, lunch menu and happy hour promotions.

Cooking your own meals: Of course, cooking your own meals will always be the cheapest way to navigate eating in London. If you have access to a kitchen in your accommodation, you could grab some groceries from **Aldi** or **Lidl** and cook your own meals. Cooking even one meal a day will greatly reduce your expenses. The butter croissants from Lidl are so, so good and perfect for breakfast.

THE PERFECT LOW-COST LONDON BUCKET LIST

* Don't take the London sightseeing bus if you're on a budget. Instead, hop on **bus number 9** (going from Hammersmith to Aldwych) or **bus number 11** (from Liverpool Street to Fulham Broadway). They still travel to all the major sites, but for a fraction of the price.

* For epic views of London, many people would tell you to visit The Shard or to take a ride on **The lastminute.com London Eye**; however, there is a way you can enjoy epic views of the skyline without the hefty price tag. Book tickets for **Sky Garden**. Known as the "walkie-talkie" building due to its shape, the top floor of this skyscraper features amazing views of London. Also, it's the highest public garden in London. I highly recommend booking before you arrive, as tickets sell out weeks in advance. Similarly, the recently opened **Horizon 22** is now London's highest free viewing platform with 360-degree views. **(Free)**

* See a **West End show**. Like New York, London has its very own Broadway called the West End. One thing I always recommend is that tourists catch a show, but you may not think this is feasible if you're on a budget. Well, here I am to the rescue! You can buy discounted tickets to numerous shows on the day of the showing at the **TKTS London booth** in Covent Garden. If you're stuck for choice, the staff gives great recommendations. If you prefer to do everything online and from the comfort of your own bed, you can also buy tickets online at the **Official London Theatre Website. ($–$$)**

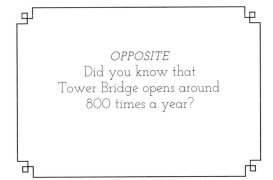

OPPOSITE
Did you know that
Tower Bridge opens around
800 times a year?

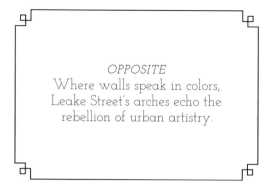

※ Leave your mark on London by doing some graffiti at **Leake Street Arches** near Waterloo. This tunnel is one of the few places in London where it is actually legal to paint the walls. **(Free)**

※ Take a **city cruise**. Board an Uber Boat by Thames **Clippers**, which is owned by Transport for London. The boat passes through many gorgeous areas of London. You can pay for both of these using your Oyster card. **($)**

※ Sticking with the theme of unique modes of transportation, try out the **IFS Cloud Cable Car** and get a bird's-eye view of London. **($)**

※ Check out some of London's breath-taking parks. London has some amazing green spaces and parks. My favorites include **Victoria Park**, **Kyoto Garden** and **Primrose Hill**. Something super special about **Richmond Park** is the **Tamsin Trail**, which is great for spotting deer! Also, watching the sunset on Primrose Hill is such a great way to end a long day of exploring. **(Free)**

※ Go on a hunt for the **Seven Noses of Soho**. Artist Rick Buckley sculpted seven noses hidden around the streets of Soho. Spend an afternoon wandering around the streets and seeing if you can spot any. **(Free)**

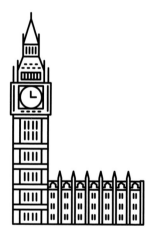

* Get lost in **London's art scene**. A trip to London isn't complete without a trip to a museum. My personal favorites are the **Tate Modern**, **Saatchi Gallery** and **National History Museum**. Fun fact: Many museums and galleries in London offer free entry to their permanent collections. This is a longstanding tradition in the city and is great for both residents and tourists to enjoy the art, culture and history of the city. **(Free)**

* Experience **afternoon tea**. If there is one thing you should know about British people, it is that we love our tea. If you are in search of an affordable afternoon tea option, check out afternoontea.co.uk for the best offers around the city. **($–$$)**

* Sit in the **Houses of Parliament Public Galleries**. The public galleries are seats in the House of Parliament, in which you can observe the proceedings of members of the houses (government officials). This is very entertaining if you happen to be lucky enough to watch on a day when they are discussing a controversial policy area. **(Free)**

* Snap some photos at Life4cuts photo booths. You get super cute and funny props to wear inside your own private photo booth and print strips to take home. **($)**

* Grab a coffee in a toilet at **The Attendant, Fitzrovia**. This coffee shop is in a former Victorian-era bathroom. Built around 1890, it was dormant for more than 50 years before it was transformed into this coffee shop. **($–$$)**

* Take a **day trip out of the city**. There are so many beautiful country-vibe sites I'm sure you'd love to see. **National Express** and **Megabus** offer great prices to locations like Oxford, The Cotswolds, Bath, Brighton and more. **($–$$)**

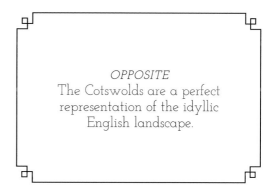

OPPOSITE
The Cotswolds are a perfect representation of the idyllic English landscape.

Paris
THE PENNY-PINCHING WAY

Paris is a city that consistently appears on the top of everyone's travel bucket list. Who doesn't love fresh pastries, beautiful artwork and breathtaking landscapes? It is no wonder that it is one of the most visited cities in the world. I have been blessed to travel there six times so far and I have every intention of returning many more times throughout my life. I fell in love with Paris on my first visit at 14 years old. My friends and I visited as part of a school trip. It was mainly supposed to be for the students studying French for GCSE; however, I talked my way onto the trip because there was no way I was going to miss experiencing the city of love with my friends. This trip was so much fun and made me fall in love with Paris for the first time, and this love has only grown over the years. In my well-traveled opinion, the "City of Lights" is one everyone must visit at least once in their lifetime.

There is just so much to see and explore! However, like the majority of popular cities in the world, it is not the cheapest. Luckily for you, dear reader, it is more than possible to visit Paris on a tighter budget if you follow some of the tips included in this chapter.

CITY PROFILE

 Currency, Bank Cards & ATMs: Similar to many other popular European cities, the euro is the currency used throughout France. You'll find that all touristy areas have ATMs, and card payments are widely accepted throughout the city. However, I still recommend you carry some cash with you for smaller retailers. One of my favorite Parisian treats is a crêpe and I find the little carts along the Seine River have the best ones, but they only accept cash. I know from experience that it is very possible to lose track of spending when it is in foreign currencies. To stop myself from spending like I have an unlimited pot of money, I usually turn on my bank notifications. This means that everything I purchase can be seen immediately in my home currency, so it makes it easier to track my spending. Also, it would be worthwhile exploring which bank cards have the lowest exchange rates and foreign transaction fees for travel. I use **Revolut** and **Monzo** for my travels, and they are a lifesaver. They have online options for anyone in the EU. Those outside of the EU might consider an online bank like **Ally Bank®**. In addition, most travel credit companies such as **Chase Bank** and **American Express** waive foreign transaction fees for users.

 Climate: The Paris climate is generally mild throughout the year. The country's hottest months are June to August. If you're traveling on a budget, you will want to avoid the peak summer season. Travel to Paris is more expensive during this time and accommodation providers raise their rates. You'll be glad to know that Paris is magical all year-round. I have visited in three different seasons and had an amazing experience each time. My last visit was during the Christmas season, and seeing all the lights and witnessing the festive ambience added a whole new dimension to my experience. My suggestion is to travel to the city in spring or autumn.

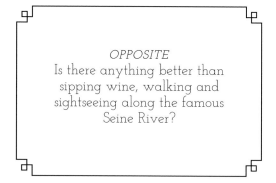

OPPOSITE
Is there anything better than sipping wine, walking and sightseeing along the famous Seine River?

 Safety: Traveling around Paris as a Black woman, I felt comfortable. The city is very diverse, so there was no staring or asking for photos (like I have experienced in many other places I have visited), although I know this may not be the same experience for everybody. I have heard a lot about some of the petty crimes in the city, such as pickpocketing and theft. Post-pandemic, these types of crimes have seen a rise in many big city tourist destinations, and Paris is no different. During my visit to Paris last year, I ran into a young lady who had had her phone swiped on the Metro. She explained that it was very quick and her phone had only been in her pocket for a few seconds. Personally, I wouldn't consider this anything to fear, but it does mean visitors should remain aware of their surroundings and protect their expensive belongings.

 Language: French is the most widely spoken language in Paris. Obvious, right? Haha. However, it should put you at ease to know that many people also speak English. It is a known cliché that the French are "rude," but that has never been my experience in Paris specifically. Paris is considered one of the most diverse cities in Europe, which makes it a melting pot of cultures and languages. My advice is to learn a few basic phrases in French before you travel to Paris.

VISITING ON A BUDGET

HOTELS & STAYS

Low budget: Paris has a range of great hostel options for those on a shoestring budget. Here are my top four hostel options for you to consider staying in on your next trip to Paris: **JO&JOE Paris Gentilly ($–$$)**, **The People Bercy ($–$$)**, **St. Christopher's Inn Paris ($–$$)** and **Generator Paris ($–$$)**.

Low to mid-budget: Choose accommodation farther away from the Eiffel Tower and other major landmarks. When I visited, I chose to stay in the budget hotel **Holiday Inn Paris Gare de L'Est Hotel** right across the street from Gare Du Nord international train station. This meant I was relatively close to everything, but I skipped the huge price that comes with hotels that have an epic view of the Eiffel Tower. A little bonus was having the Metro entrance five steps from the lobby of my hotel. Some of my other suggestions include **Hotel Leopold** in the 14th Arrondissement, **Mama Shelter** in the 20th Arrondissement and staying in the 18th Arrondissement.

Mid-budget: Another option is to stay in an Airbnb outside of central Paris. Staying in an apartment on the outskirts of Paris in the same building as locals could be an immersive alternative. On my last visit to Paris I stayed in an Airbnb a stone's throw away from La Défense and it cost one-third of the price of other apartments I looked at closer to the center.

TRANSPORTATION

Getting there: Let's start with getting to Paris. **Omio** is a good website to use for comparing the best travel deals to get to Paris. This covers planes, buses and trains. For those of us who live in Europe, the train isn't always the most cost-effective way to visit Paris if you're booking closer to the time of the trip.

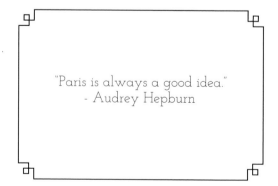

"Paris is always a good idea."
- Audrey Hepburn

Trains and buses: Now on to getting around the city. Paris has great transport links and a well-established public transportation system. The city is split into different zones, which makes the train and bus systems easy to navigate. Tickets are inexpensive, which makes this the best way to travel around the city cheaply. One of my favorite things about using the system is how fast it is to reach different attractions. A little **tip:** You'll want to take the **Metro line 6** between the stops Passy and Bir-Hakeim to see unbeatable views of Paris, especially the Eiffel Tower. Thank me later!

An even bigger **tip:** If you're only spending a few days in Paris, don't buy individual Metro tickets! Instead, buy a pack of ten Metro tickets for 15 percent off. Alternatively, the Paris transport card may be more beneficial to you depending on your plans. The card will give you unlimited travel on the bus, Metro, tramway and RER networks and its suburbs. You can choose from one-, two-, three- or five-day passes. Just be sure to check which zones you have access to, as you'll want Zones 1 to 3 for the city center and nearby suburbs.

If you're staying for a week or more, you should consider getting the **Navigo Découverte Travel Card**. This card allows unlimited transport to and from the airport, Disneyland Paris, Palace of Versailles and all around the city. To purchase it, go to any Metro ticket office in Paris with a passport-size photo and pay a few dollars for the card.

FOOD & DRINK

Don't eat at restaurants near main attractions. Instead, use **TheFork** app to get up to 50 percent off delicious restaurants farther away from the monuments. You'll find much cheaper restaurants wandering through the back streets of Paris and eating with local Parisians. A few great restaurants to try featured on the app include **Les Rupins**, **Pizza Pizze** and **Cheesers Food Truck**.

Take advantage of the bakeries. One of the absolute best things about Paris is its bakeries. I can personally confirm I ate my fair share of breads, pastries and deli items. The nice thing about this is not only is everything affordable, but it's also filling! I can get a large croissant and a deli sandwich and eat that for breakfast and lunch, avoiding spending too much at restaurants before dinner. If you are an *Emily in Paris* fan, then you have to visit **La Boulangerie Moderne**. This is the bakery that Emily visited just outside of her flat in Season 1, Epi-

sode 1, and I can confirm the baked goods here taste absolutely divine! Some other must-try bakeries are **Land&Monkeys Beaumarchais**, **BO&MIE** and **Mamiche**. If you visit Mamiche, be sure to get the orange blossom brioche! However, don't worry if you are short on time and not able to make it to any of these. If there's one thing Paris does well, it's baked delights.

If takeaway food is more your style, use the **Too Good to Go** app to purchase food for half price or less from a range of establishments. Food waste is one of the great challenges of our time, and the Too Good to Go app is one way to contribute to a solution, while benefiting from some discounted tasty food. The app provides an overview of shops and restaurants in any area that have surplus food. Those outlets put together a surprise bag of food at a lower price and you can order it right within the app. One of my favorite things to do is people watch, which is the perfect underrated activity to do while nibbling on a bargain lunch.

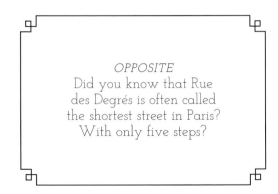

OPPOSITE
Did you know that Rue des Degrés is often called the shortest street in Paris? With only five steps?

THE PERFECT LOW-COST PARIS BUCKET LIST

❋ You can view the **Eiffel Tower**, **Arc de Triomphe** and the **Louvre** Museum for **FREE** if you don't mind admiring the architecture from the outside. I can already hear you saying, "But, Tonia! I want to see what it's like from the inside." I got you. Did you know that many attractions in Paris are cheaper if you visit at night and buy tickets on the official website? Each monument is beautifully lit up at night and still just as fantastic to visit.

❋ In addition, many popular museums in Paris are **free** on the first Sunday of the month. Some examples are **Musée National d'Art Moderne**, **Musée des Arts et Métiers**, **Musée de la Chasse et de la Nature** and **Musée National de l'Orangerie**. In addition, EU residents under 26 have free access to all national museums in France, including famous places like the **Louvre** Museum and **Musée d'Orsay**.

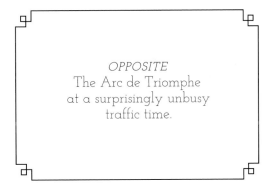

OPPOSITE
The Arc de Triomphe
at a surprisingly unbusy
traffic time.

* Discover the hidden gems of **Montmartre**. The 18th Arrondissement of Paris has become much more popular within the last few years, with good reason. Exploring the neighborhood is like walking into a Parisian picture book; you could easily spend an entire day wandering through the streets. The area is home to the stunning **Sacré-Cœur Basilica (free to enter)** and many other small museums for those looking for unique things to do in Paris.

* For a unique activity, check out **Fotoautomat**. This is one of the best photo booth locations in Paris. **($)**

* Go **teddy bear spotting**. In 2018, book shop owners began lending out large teddy bears to establishments all across the city for them to display. These bears are called Les Nounours des Gobelins. Spend an afternoon seeing if you can spot any of these bears. Hint: Be sure to check café tables carefully, but these bears can be found in many unexpected places. If you enjoy puzzles and scavenger hunts, this is the perfect activity for you. **(Free)**

* Take a day trip to the **Palace of Versailles**. As a lover of history, visiting the location where the post–World War I treaty was signed was a complete "pinch me" moment. You can bask in the grandeur of the **Hall of Mirrors ($–$$)** where the treaty was actually signed. If you live in Europe and are under 26, call yourself extremely lucky, as you can get free access to all the decadent chambers of the royals. I am indeed very jealous! If you are a non-EU resident and are under 18, you get free entry on the first Sunday of every month between November and March. This includes entry to the entire estate, including the Palace of Versailles and the **Estate of Trianon**.

OPPOSITE
Montmartre is the artistic hub all creatives need to visit.

* One of my favorite things to do when visiting a new city is go on a **walking tour**. I find it a great way to learn more about a city and experience daily life there. Many cities across the world (including Paris) offer free walking tours. **Context Travel Tours** and **Paris Greeters** are two organizations that offer this service. If you're looking to enjoy Paris like a local, this is the perfect way to do it. **(Free, discretionary tip)**

* Visit the oldest still operating market in Paris. Marché des Enfants Rouges is located in the 3rd Arrondissement. The various shopping stands offer cheeses, fruits, wine, flowers and more, and you can grab a coffee for as little as **$2**.

* Visit one of the **Pierre Hermés stores** and taste the best macarons in Paris. They have a huge selection of amazing macarons and each one costs a few dollars. Of course, I have a macaron scandal story for you to sweeten the suggestion; let's call it "macaron gate." On one of my previous trips to Paris I visited **Ladurée café** and posted on my Instagram stories that I loved the macarons I purchased there so much that they could potentially be the best in Paris (a bold statement, I know). Of course I was swiftly corrected by my many Parisian followers that I needed to visit **Pierre Hermé** before making such a ludicrous statement. I can confirm that they were all completely right and I did indeed bow my head in shame. Fortunately, I made this school girl error so you don't have to; no need to thank me! The power of social media, aye!

* Go to the **Galeries Lafayette** and enjoy the perfect rooftop view. One thing about Paris is there are so many amazing places to enjoy the view and this is one of the best! **(Free)**

* The famous **Notre-Dame** cathedral lies on its own island in the middle of the Seine accessible by *pont* (bridge). Although the entrance to the tower itself is not free, the rest of the cathedral is. It is widely regarded as one of the most beautiful examples of gothic architecture in the world. A note that Notre-Dame is currently under construction due to the fire in 2019, and is due to reopen in December 2024. **(Free)**

* See the sunrise/sunset at **Trocadéro building**. Paris isn't exactly known for its sunsets, but one of the most beautiful sunsets I have seen to date was in Paris on a random July evening. The sky was filled with vibrant orange, reds and purples. It was truly a vision. Trocadéro's proximity to the Eiffel Tower and its eastward position makes it a prime sunset spot. **(Free)**

* Stroll around the **Tuileries Garden**. Home to the **Musée de l'Orangerie** that displays Monet's lilies. This gorgeous garden is the perfect place to appreciate the beauty of nature with a pond water feature in the center of the park. This is a great location to feed the ducks and people watch. If you are fortunate enough to be enjoying Paris in the winter season, visiting this park is a must as it's home to the Tuileries Garden Christmas market, **La Magie de Noël**. It's the biggest, the liveliest, the loudest and the most fun-filled Christmas market in the city. The market is packed with affordable fair rides, gifts and crafts as well as mouth-watering snacking and dining options.

* Window-shop on **Champs-Élysées**, an iconic avenue in Paris that connects the Arc de Triomphe and the Place de la Concorde. It is home to many luxury stores and decadent restaurants. **(Free)**

* Stroll along the **Seine River**. The Seine is an iconic part of Paris, which makes it the perfect place to unwind and share a bottle of wine with a friend. **(Free)**

Iceland
REYKJAVIK AND BEYOND!

Let's embark on a journey to the land of fire and ice that is Iceland, where breathtaking landscapes, glaciers, active volcanos, waterfalls, geothermal pools and beautiful hikes await your arrival. Sounds pretty dreamy, right? I am genuinely so happy to write this chapter, because out of the 60 countries I have visited to date, I can say with confidence that Iceland is my favorite. Furthermore, it's also a favorite among many of my friends and colleagues in the travel industry. I always find it hard to describe exactly why I think this, or how my trip made me feel, but of course for you, my beloved reader, I will give it a shot.

At heart, I am 100 percent a nature girl. I love fresh air, swimming in natural waters, seeing unreal landscapes and hiking. Iceland provides everything that I need to feed my soul. Unfortunately, Iceland's allure is often accompanied by a perception of high costs, which can deter budget-conscious adventurers. To an extent, this perception is true; Iceland is the most expensive country I have ever visited—I mean eye-wateringly expensive. However, through thoughtful planning, tips and a dash of creativity, an affordable Icelandic adventure is more than possible and incredibly rewarding.

CITY PROFILE

Currency, Bank Cards & ATMs: The currency used in Iceland is the Icelandic króna. During both of my trips to Iceland, I never withdrew any cash. Card payments are widely accepted across the country and the Icelandic people tend to pay for almost everything with bank cards. However, you will need a card that uses a chip and a pin. Mastercard and Visa are both widely accepted.

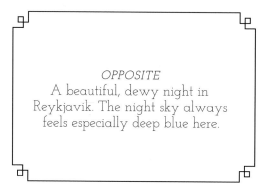

OPPOSITE
A beautiful, dewy night in Reykjavik. The night sky always feels especially deep blue here.

PASSPORT

Climate: Iceland has relatively cool temperatures all year-round due to its location, so if you're looking for a sunny, hot experience, this probably isn't the right location for that. However, during my first trip here, I embarked on a two-hour hike in a sweater thinking I would be cold, but ended up feeling like I was on fire because the sun was beaming. All this to say, layer up and adjust what you're wearing to the temperature. My preference for visiting Iceland will always be summer (June to August), as it offers the mildest temperatures. I prefer trying to avoid the icy roads, strong winds and freezing temperatures. Did you know that during summer, Iceland has 24 hours of sunshine? This is the perfect opportunity for you to maximize your days by exploring during the night. If the summer prices are over your budget, consider visiting in the autumn (September to October). If your dream is to see the northern lights, then your best bet would be visiting in the winter (October to April) and braving the cold.

Safety: Let's keep this short. Iceland is considered very safe; you have nothing to worry about. The country boasts a low crime rate and a welcoming and friendly population. This makes Iceland the perfect destination for a first-time solo traveler. During my first trip to Iceland, my friend and I ended up picking up a hitchhiker at the gas station for a four-hour road trip. On another occasion, we were glamping in a dome tent, where the tent opening didn't lock, and never had a worry. As a caveat, I am not actively encouraging you to do this, but these are just examples of how comfortable and safe we felt exploring the country. Of course, no country is completely crime-free and it's good practice to exercise reasonable caution.

On the other hand, while Iceland's natural landscapes are stunning, they can also present some hazards. Rapidly changing weather, unstable volcanoes and geothermal areas can pose a risk. Just make sure you are checking weather conditions and respecting safety warnings. Although Iceland really is the perfect destination for the solo traveler, because of its impeccable safety record, traveling with a friend means you'll be able to split the costs of things like a camper van, rental car, hotel stays, groceries, etc. If you are determined to visit solo, don't let the prices scare you off; you'll just need to have a flexible budget, that's all!

 Language: The main language spoken in Iceland is Icelandic, as well as English.

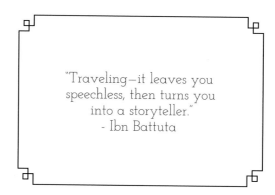

"Traveling—it leaves you speechless, then turns you into a storyteller."
- Ibn Battuta

VISITING ON A BUDGET

HOTEL & STAYS

Camper van: Budget travelers who would like to venture out of Reykjavik and see more of the remote hidden gems of the country should rent a camper van. Iceland's rugged terrain and remote location makes accommodations a challenge. Having a camper van means accommodation, transport and food costs are all reduced simultaneously, not to mention the freedom and schedule flexibility. You can rent a camper van with ample sleeping room, a small kitchen, storage and sometimes even full shower facilities. In a country where the road trip journey is just as important as the destination itself, renting a camper van is invaluable. For the first time this year, I rented a camper van for one of my trips and the feeling was so liberating. I was able to park and wake up in front of breathtaking landscapes just outside my window, and there is no feeling quite like it. Just picture the northern lights dancing around the sky as you sleep or waking up next to a jaw-dropping waterfall. You can use sites like **Go See Travel**, **Campervan Iceland** and **Motorhome Republic** to search for the best rental deals. Some great providers you should consider are **CampEasy Iceland ($–$$$)**, **Happy Campers ($–$$)**, **Hertz ($–$$)** or **Lava Car Rental ($–$$)**.

Low budget: For shorter visits, where you plan to be based in Reykjavik and take day trips, opting for a hostel is a good idea for those on a budget. **KEX Hostel ($$)** is often a top option for budget travelers because of its fun atmosphere and stylish design. **Hlemmur Square Hotel & Hostel ($)** has a central location, modern design and restaurant and bar facilities. Other good options include **Reykjavik Downtown Hi Hostel ($$)**, **Galaxy Pod Hostel ($$)** and **Bus Hostel Reykjavik ($$)**. All great vibes, clean and budget friendly.

Bed-and-breakfast/guesthouses: Staying in a bed-and-breakfast gives you tremendous value for your money as you get a meal and a range of amenities that may cost extra when staying at other hotels. I suggest either **Sunna Guesthouse ($$–$$$)** or **Gestinn Guesthouse ($$)**.

Mid-budget: Great value for hotel options are **Fosshotel Reykjavik ($$$)**, which is one of the largest hotels in Reykjavik and is popular for its modern decor and convenient location; **CenterHotel Plaza**, with its prime location in downtown **($$–$$$)**; and **Storm Hotel by Keahotels ($–$$)**, which boasts an inviting, minimalist design. All are located near the city center. Another option slightly farther afield is **Icelandair Hotel Reykjavik Natura ($$$)**, whose design is inspired by Iceland's natural landscapes.

Camping: If you're an adventurous traveler, like my hitchhiking friend I mentioned earlier, you may want to consider wild camping. Many campsites offer basic facilities, stunning views and budget-friendly prices.

TRANSPORTATION

Getting there: Consider visiting Iceland on a layover. If you are flying into Europe using Icelandair, they offer several short layovers. This is a great opportunity to see some of the world's top travel destination for a few days, without the extra flight costs.

Car rentals: I highly recommend renting a car when visiting Iceland. Some of Iceland's most breathtaking sights are located a great distance from the city center and are often in remote locations. Public transport in Iceland is limited, particularly if you are planning on visiting in the off-season when many routes are closed. Also, tours can be very expensive, so renting a car means your transportation options are not limited. I used **Rentalcars.com** when I rented a car in Iceland. It's a good source to see the cheapest rates, receive good service and find access to discounts.

FOOD & DRINK

Supermarkets: When I arrived in Iceland, the first thing I did after picking up my rental car was head to the nearest major supermarket on my itinerary route. This was **Krónan** grocery store. Not to scare you, but I have never seen groceries this expensive in my entire existence. Funnily enough, this was still the cheapest option for most of my meals. If you are on a budget in Iceland, you should be aiming to make 75 to 90 percent of your own meals.

Restaurants: Iceland isn't really known for its food, but on the occasions when I ate out, I had several delicious eats while I was there that I must shout out. Trying a hot dog from **Bæjarins Beztu Pylsur** is a must. I loved it so much I returned a few minutes later to buy a second one. It's inexpensive, tasty and stays open late. **Skyr** yogurt is also a delicious traditional yogurt, perfect for a light breakfast. Download the **Icelandic Coupons** app for discounts on a few restaurants and attractions.

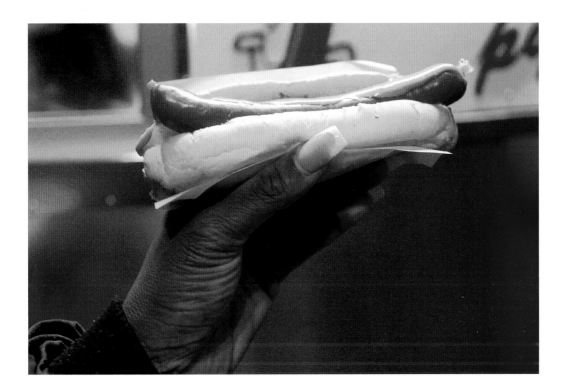

Drinks: Drink the tap water! Iceland has some of the world's best water, and you can drink straight from the tap or even streams. On the other hand, if you are planning to enjoy some alcoholic drinks, you will want to purchase these from the airport duty free. In Iceland, alcohol is heavily taxed and needs to be bought in special shops called *vinbudin*, which are run by the government, and they typically only open from 11 a.m. to 6 p.m.

ABOVE
The famous, much-loved hot dog, in all of its glory. Don't skip this!

THE PERFECT LOW-COST ICELAND BUCKET LIST

❋ See the **Sun Voyager** sculpture. It's a huge, natural sculpture that is in the middle of Reykjavik. It's a dream boat and an ode to the sun, which represents the promise of undiscovered territory and a dream of hope, progress and freedom in Iceland. You can go any time of the day to see it and there is no fee. **(Free)**

❋ Drive the **Golden Circle** route, one of Iceland's most famous routes. There are many natural wonders along the way to stop and gasp at. You'll be able to see geysers, waterfalls, a national park and much more on your journey. The most affordable way to see these marvels is to drive around the route on your own and only pay the small entry fees. There are tours available, but taking one would be the pricier option. **($)**

❋ Check out **Kerið Crater Lake** to see what a collapsed volcano looks like. The crater is approximately 3,000 years old and offers a stunning landscape. **($)**

❋ See the diamonds on **Diamond Beach**, making sure to stop off at **Jökulsárlón Glacier Lagoon**. Seeing the crystal-clear icebergs resting on the jet-black sand is quite the must-see spectacle. When I visited, there was even an iceberg big enough for me to sit on and take super unique photos. **(Free)**

❋ **Explore Reykjavik's street art scene.** As you stroll through the city streets you are greeted by murals bursting with vibrant colors and creativity as well as vivid portraits with abstract designs. **(Free)**

OPPOSITE
Did you know that Iceland is almost entirely mosquito-free, due to its climate and cool temperatures? You can hike free of pests!

* Visit **Reynisfjara black sand beach**. Reynisfjara jet-black sands were formed from volcanic activity, making it one of the most epic beaches you can visit in the world. The sight of the beach carries into the horizon and is a true testament to the beauty of nature's architecture. **(Free)**

* Snap photos with an **Icelandic horse**. These horses are stunning and unique to the country. They can be found in fields alone on the side of the road as you drive around the country. **(Free)**

* See active hot lava at **Fagradalsfjall volcano**. Each summer for the last three years this volcano has erupted. If you're lucky enough to be visiting Iceland during this time, seeing the active lava is a must. This is truly a once-in-a-lifetime experience. **(Free)**

* Wander around **Elliðaárdalur Valley**, a true hidden gem near Reykjavik. It's most known for its beautiful **Elliðaá river**, which runs through the entire valley and features quaint little waterfalls. **($)**

ABOVE
Icelandic horses: small in stature, immense in spirit.

* See the remains of the **Sólheimasandur plane crash**. The US DC-3 airplane wreck is popular because of the visual contrast between the shell of the craft and the background landscape. **($)**

* Go **hiking to see a waterfall**. Iceland is a hiker's paradise, and there's literally a hiking opportunity around every corner. I really enjoyed the hikes to **Glymur waterfall** and **Svartifoss waterfall**. **($)**

* Watch the sunset at **Seljalandsfoss waterfall**. One unique thing about this waterfall is that you can walk behind it. Watching the sunset from this spot is truly breathtaking—just make sure you bring a waterproof jacket. **(Free)**

* Visit **hot springs**. Iceland is known for its geothermal activity, which means it has amazing hot springs. This is the perfect way to relax and rejuvenate after a long day. One of the most famous ones is the **Blue Lagoon**; however, nearby more affordable options are **Vesturbæjarlaug Pool**, **Kvika Footbath** and **Reykjadalur Hot Spring Thermal River**. **($)**

ABOVE
I got lucky and saw an active geyser during my trip! Keep your eyes peeled for natural wonders all around you here.

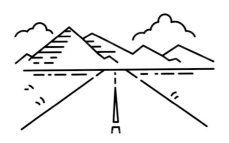

Rome
THE PURSE-FRIENDLY APPROACH

Italy is a must-visit country. There, I said it. Hear me out! There are numerous reasons why it is one of the most visited destinations in Europe. From the historical grandeur of Rome to the romantic canals of Venice, from the picturesque Alps surrounding Lake Como to the sun-soaked Amalfi Coast, the appeal of Italy is undeniable.

I have been to Italy several times so far, and I feel like I haven't even scratched the surface of all the architectural marvels, artistic treasures or culinary delights. My favorite places so far have been Rome, Venice and Lake Como, but there are so many highlights across the country and still many places on my bucket list. I always love cities where the timeless beauty of ancient architecture is seamlessly blended into the modern landscape. Random fun fact, but for those who haven't visited:

The Colosseum is located smack bang in the middle of Rome. I literally turned a corner and there it was. I always assumed iconic monuments like this would be out of the way in a remote area, but on many occasions this has not been the case. In addition, Italy is the birthplace of many irresistible dishes. Pasta is probably my favorite food in the entire world, so when I was in Italy, I was in food heaven.

Italy has so much to offer every single kind of traveler and it is one of the gems of Europe. However, experiencing the splendors of Italy does not have to mean you spend your life savings on the trip of a lifetime. We're going to get into some great ways you can experience everything Europe has to offer, while remaining a budget-savvy traveler.

CITY PROFILE

 Currency, Bank Cards & ATMs: Unsurprisingly, the currency used in Italy is the euro (EUR). Mastercard and Visa are widely accepted in Italy and a few select establishments accept American Express. Similarly to London, in many major cities such as Rome, contactless payments are accepted. Just make sure that the card connected to your online wallet is one that doesn't charge for international transaction fees, like the **Chase Sapphire Preferred Card** or **Capital One 360**. Unlike some other places on the continent, it's worth noting that if you are in a bind, a few businesses in tourist-heavy areas may accept the US dollar. I wouldn't rely on this, but it is always worth asking. If you are planning to visit more remote towns and villages like Matera or Gangi, cash payments remain the preferred method of payment due to local preferences. (These towns often offer a glimpse into the traditional and authentic Italian way of life, so it's worth it to visit them one day. You may be pleased to know that tourism has increased greatly in these areas over the years, so the current situation may change soon.) Moving on to ATMs, they are widely available across cities, many smaller towns and train stations. My advice is to try and withdraw all the cash you'll need for your trip in one go to avoid any ATM fees. Also, it'll save you from having to run around looking for ATMs, which has happened to me on many occasions, so I can tell you with all certainty it's the worst.

 Climate: The most inexpensive time to visit Italy is in the winter (December to February). Weather along the Mediterranean coast is mild, which makes it a great time to visit cities like Venice and Florence with reduced crowds and lower hotel rates. If you need more convincing, it's also the perfect climate to enjoy some of Italy's hearty warm dishes, such as risottos and filling stews. By embracing the magic of winter, you can save significant amounts on your trip. In all honesty, visiting Italy in the summer is a beautiful, special experience, and fortunately for those of us invested in affordable travel, the warmth of the summer months continues to linger into September and October. This is the perfect way to enjoy the great weather without the hefty summer

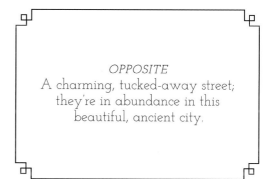

OPPOSITE
A charming, tucked-away street; they're in abundance in this beautiful, ancient city.

price tags. I visited Venice once in September and I must say it was very crowded. I still had a great time, but navigating the narrow streets was a little challenging at the time. However, this was just after pandemic restrictions had loosened and there was a sudden burst of people traveling, but rest assured, there's no place like Italy in the summer, even if it is crowded.

Safety: Italy is generally safe to visit as a group and as a solo traveler. One thing to be aware of is pickpockets and petty crime. My opinion on visiting Italy as a Black woman is split. Starting with the positives, I have never had a bad experience on my many trips to this gorgeous country. In addition, I would say no one I know personally has had a bad experience. However, if you're a chronic social media addict like I am, you have probably come across many people of color who did not enjoy their experiences and said they were treated poorly because of their race. I have not yet heard any stories of people feeling unsafe, just that they felt very unwelcome. Cities like Rome and Venice have been popular tourist spots for years, but as more remote areas become popular and open more to tourism, there is still work to be done in terms of people educating themselves and removing the prejudices they have about other races. This is something to take into consideration when deciding to visit and planning your trip.

Language: The official language of Italy is Italian. It's spoken widely throughout Italy. While many Italians in more popular tourist areas have a working knowledge of English, it is slightly less common in more rural areas. Hence, I recommend you familiarize yourself with key phrases before your trip. A free app you can use to begin learning some key travel phrases is **Duolingo**. The app is free to download, and the basic package is free to use. When I was visiting Guatemala a few years ago, I knew English was not widely spoken in the smaller towns around Lake Atitlán. So, a few months before I was due to fly out, I began using Duolingo to learn some basic Spanish so I could connect with locals as a solo traveler. To my shock, this turned out to be an immensely useful skill. I realized even within the short amount of time using the app that I had learned much more than I thought and was able to hold some good conversations. I was able to learn about some hidden gems tourists don't usually visit, given discounts and had a local person keep me company for some meals. This is definitely an advantage you will want in Italy!

VISITING ON A BUDGET

HOTEL & STAYS

Low budget: Affordable accommodation options in Rome are located close to the Roma Termini station; although slightly on the outskirts of the city, it's a great option for balancing being central-ish and staying within budget. **The RomeHello Hostel ($–$$)** is a cool hostel that is affordable and central. It's only a short walk to hot spots such as the Trevi Fountain and the Pantheon. The walls are decorated in graffiti, so it's really a unique stay. **YellowSquare Rome ($–$$)** is one of Rome's most famous hostels because of its social events; it's also conveniently located. Other good affordable options include **Generator Rome ($)**, **Palladini Hostel ($)**, **The Beehive Hotel & Hostel ($–$$)** and **Alessandro Palace & Bar ($–$$)**.

Mid-budget: My suggestions for good mid-range hotels are as follows: **Hotel Artemide ($$)** offers an affordable luxury stay, with key features being a rooftop terrace with a hot tub. **Hotel Quirinale ($$)** has very spacious rooms (which is something I always look for when booking a hotel) and is located within walking distance to the Trevi Fountain. This was great for getting those 5 a.m. empty-ish photos. **Top Floor Colosseo Guesthouse ($$)** has beautifully designed rooms close to the Colosseum. Lastly, **Residenza Venti Settembre ($$)** is a family-owned hotel that offers great personal service.

ABOVE
Staying in a modern hostel in the heart of an ancient city is the best kind of juxtaposition.

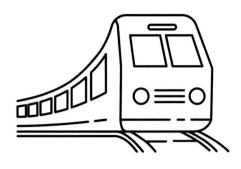

Public transportation: Getting around larger cities like Rome can easily be done by public transport such as the Metro or bus. You can take a ride for only a few dollars and, coupled with walking to a few key spots, this is the most cost-effective way to navigate the city.

Walking: When I was in Rome, I spent the majority of my time walking between some of the major sites. I found it to be the easiest and best way to get around, and not to mention free. Walking in Rome during any time of day is pretty magical. One of the best ways to get the most out of the city is to wake up super early and walk along the empty streets. There is something otherworldly about seeing Rome bathed in the light of dawn. Walking everywhere also means you won't feel guilty about indulging in excessive amounts of gelato and pasta.

TRANSPORTATION

Intercity transportation: Getting around Italy is significantly easier than some other European countries because of their extensive and state-run train network. Although more expensive, the high-speed train option means you can get from one side of the country to the other in a few short hours. These are often referred to as **Frecciarossa, Frecciargento** or **Frecciabianca**. Also, they have a streamlined front design and are typically bold in color (red, silver or white). A more budget-friendly option is the regional trains. I highly recommend visiting more than one city during your trip to Italy, and the high-speed train is the perfect way to do this. Consider spending a day or two in Venice. You can book this on the **12Go** app or directly with the train lines.

OPPOSITE
There is nothing better than getting lost in Rome's scenic street scenes, and wandering into a wine bar for the afternoon.

FOOD & DRINK

Did you know that each Italian city has its own specialty dish? The Roman classic cacio e pepe, which is basically a salt-and-pepper creamy pasta, is a must-try when in the city. A great place to try this, recommended by my Roman friend, is **Osteria da Fortunata ($)**, as the prices are affordable for Rome and you can watch the pasta being freshly made in the front window. Another Roman delight to sample here is trapizzino, which is like a calzone folded and stuffed with different Roman delicacies. Like Paris, use **TheFork app** to get up to 50 percent off delicious restaurants farther away from the monuments.

Here is a list of some of the best cheap eats in Rome: **Pinsere** serves amazing pinsa, which is an ancient type of pizza that costs around $8. They offer a great selection and this delight is perfect for lunch or dinner; just grab a pinsa and head to the nearest bench to people watch. **Forno Campo de' Fiori** is most known for their pizza bianco, which is essentially a plain dough "white" pizza with delicious toppings, costing around $8. Moving on to my favorite dish: pasta. **Trattoria Vecchia Roma** portion sizes are generous, with each dish costing less than $12. Last but not least, **Pastificio Guerra** prepares freshly cooked pasta dishes every day for under $7. For lunch, they offer one of the best deals you'll find in Rome.

Here are my tips on how to spot authentic gelato. Rule 1: The container the gelato is in will be flat and/or have a lid. If you see big mounds, the gelato has been whisked with air, so you'll be paying for air. Rule 2: Look for these three flavors: banana (the color should be off-white), pistachio (should be an earthy, dull color, not turtle green) and mint (should be light green and not glowing in the dark). Rule 3: The shop should not have too many flavors. If there are too many options, the gelato can't be homemade and must be industrially produced. Rule 4: If you enter a gelato shop and one is fake, it means they all are. Happy eating!

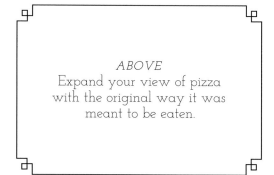

ABOVE
Expand your view of pizza with the original way it was meant to be eaten.

THE PERFECT LOW-COST ROME BUCKET LIST

※ Visit **Villa Borghese**. Here, you should rent a small boat and enjoy the lake for an afternoon. It's such a cute, wholesome activity and the perfect place for a stroll and picnic. Also, you can rent an **electric Rosaline bike** and cycle around the beautiful gardens. **($)**

BELOW
Don't skip out on renting a boat here. You'll float in the sunshine on the most idyllic afternoon of your life.

✳ You cannot visit Rome without seeing the **Colosseum**, but since you're on a budget, did you know that the Colosseum, **Roman Forum** and **Palatine Hill** are all free to enter on the first Sunday of the month? Similarly, the **Vatican museums** can be seen for free on the last Sunday of the month. You'll want to visit all these sights first thing in the morning before the lines pick up and the wait times increase. **(Free)**

✳ Look at priceless art in **Basilica Parrocchiale Santa Maria del Popolo**. This is home to some of the most incredible pieces of art in all of Rome, including artists such as Bernini, Caravaggio and Raphael. Another great place to see artwork is **San Luigi Dei Francesi** near the Pantheon. Here, you can find a series of paintings by the famous artist Caravaggio. These are both such hidden gems and honestly so easy to miss. Unfortunately, the Basilica is currently closed for restoration until November 2024, but if you visit beyond that, it's a must-see. **(Free)**

✳ Check out excellent views of the city at **Castel Sant'Angelo**. Be warned, you will have to climb up a lot of stairs, but the view at the end is worth it. **($)**

✳ Grab a takeaway cocktail from **Taberna**. Taberna is a hole-in-the-wall type of establishment and they sell delicious $6 cocktails in a cup. It's the perfect way to cool down after battling the crowds to throw your coin into the fountain. **($)**

✳ See the BEST view of **St. Stephen's Basilica**: The **Knights of Malta keyhole** has become quite popular over the years, but many people still don't know about it. When you look through the small hole you will see a perfectly framed view of St. Stephen's Basilica. **(Free)**

✳ See if you can survive the **CUBE**: Okay, so this is slightly on the pricier end of activities to do in Rome, but it was so much fun I had to slide it in anyway. **CUBE Challenges** has 26 rooms filled with different challenges to test your skills and strength. **($$)**

The Greek Isles

ISLAND HOPPING WITHOUT THE HEFTY PRICE TAG

Being able to visit the Greek islands is a dream shared by many people across the world. I'm sure by now you must have seen photos of the iconic whitewashed buildings, blue domes and women wearing long dresses flowing in the wind. Greece is made up of 6,000 islands and islets scattered in the Greek seas, of which 227 islands are inhabited, so you really are spoiled for choice with options on where you'd like to soak in the warm Mediterranean sun. Some islands are known for their architecture, some for their unique beaches and natural features, and others for their cosmopolitan vibe and acclaimed nightlife (I am looking at you, Mykonos!).

My first trip to Greece was to explore the Cyclades island of Santorini. Since then, I have returned numerous times, with my latest trip being to the gorgeous island of Rhodes. Let's address the elephant in the room: Greece being expensive to visit is a common misconception. What people mean when they say this is that the most popular islands, Santorini and Mykonos, are considered pricey, as previously mentioned, but there is so much choice. I promise you, other islands are just as stunning as these and much more friendly to your bank account. I plan to convince you to consider basing yourself on one of these other amazing islands and taking a day trip to visit Santorini or Mykonos (if you must); more on how to do this later. When you finish this chapter, you'll be equipped with everything you need to live out your *Mamma Mia!* dreams.

CITY PROFILE

 Currency, Bank Cards & ATMs: The official currency in Greece is the euro (EUR); are you beginning to sense a pattern here? Unlike many other cities previously explored in this book, I recommend having a mix of payment types at your disposal, which is what I have done each time I have visited. Mastercard and Visa are widely accepted at major establishments, but it's wise to carry some euro cash on hand, particularly for smaller eateries or places that only allow card payments if a minimum is spent. ATMs are readily available on most islands, including the ones that will be mentioned in this deep dive.

 Climate: In my opinion, the best time to visit Greece is September to October. The weather is perfect for water activities, the summer crowds have begun to disperse and you should have no problems finding affordable accommodation and activities. Also, I find it quite difficult to explore thoroughly when it's too hot (over 100°F [38°C]), so my preference is the colder season, when the heat is more subdued.

 Safety: I felt super safe as a Black woman exploring the Greek islands. Every time I visit, I feel incredibly welcomed and have never had any issues. Generally, I have heard great things from my fellow travelers who have visited the islands. Although, please remember that each island is not a monolith. I once read a blog post from a Black traveler who visited on a girls' trip and felt they were treated with bias on the island on Mykonos. For example, it was assumed they were unable to pay for fancier restaurants or purchase things in designer shops. Unfortunately, many Black travelers are all too familiar with the anxiety surrounding visiting new places and facing hyper-surveillance in circumstances like this. I don't share this story with you to scare you off, but to provide the most balanced experiences I can with the knowledge I have. If there is only one thing you take away from this book, it should be that you shouldn't let fear stop you from experiencing the world to the fullest. I have found Greek hospitality to be impeccable, and I am very excited for you to experience the warm kindness of the islands.

 Language: It might seem slightly obvious, but I will say it anyway: the official language spoken in Greece is Greek. The tourism industry in Greece is well equipped to accommodate international guests, with many locals speaking English. Essential information in major tourist areas is also provided in English, making it relatively easy to navigate and communicate during your travels. As always, I recommend learning a few key phrases, and here are a few to start you off: *kaliméra* (good morning), *efcharistó* (thank you), *parakaló* (please) and my personal favorite, *Poú eínai ta kalýtera fotografiká simeía?* (Where are the best photo spots?)

ABOVE
I love the colors of this country. You can get lost in the aquamarine sea, then explore the endless lush green landscape.

VISITING ON A BUDGET

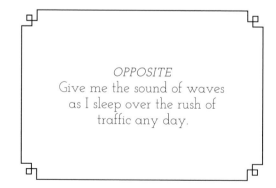

HOTEL & STAYS

Rhodes

Low budget: Standout hostels in Rhodes are **STAY Hostel Rhodes ($)**, which opened in 2022 and has a relaxing vibe and aesthetic. They offer a range of social spaces and pride themselves on their community feel. The cozy apartment suites of **Annapolis Inn ($)** and **Rhodes Youth Hostel ($)** are ideally located in the center of Rhodes Town and close to where all the action is.

Mid-budget: For the budget-savvy traveler, Rhodes Town is an ideal base because it has diverse accommodations and good access links to the beach, local attractions and restaurants. It's great that budget consciousness does not have to come at the expense of being comfortable. Some great options are **Mitsis Petit Palais Beach Hotel ($–$$)**, **Lomeniz Hotel ($–$$)** and **Hotel Mediterranean ($$)**. Furthermore, for travelers looking for a slightly larger complex offering, **Sun Beach Resort Complex ($–$$)** in Ialysos is another gem. On my most recent visit to Rhodes, I stayed at the **Sheraton Rhodes Resort ($$–$$$)** and loved everything about it.

Corfu

Low budget: Corfu welcomes budget travelers with a range of hostel options for an affordable stay. My favorites are the world-famous **Pink Palace ($)**, which has been drawing international adventurous travelers for years, **Corfu Backpackers Beach Hostel ($)** and **Angelica's Backpacker's Hostel ($)**.

Mid-budget: There are a plethora of appealing midrange hotel options waiting for you in Corfu. Similar to Rhodes, Corfu Town is the prime choice to base yourself in, with its charming streets and cultural significance. Standout accommodations are **Mon Repos Palace ($$)** and **Hotel Bretagne ($$)**. If you don't mind staying a little farther out, **Aeolos Beach Resort ($$)** and **Blue Princess Beach Resort ($$–$$$)** are good alternatives.

OPPOSITE
Give me the sound of waves as I sleep over the rush of traffic any day.

TRANSPORTATION

Getting there: When deciding how to enter the country, it's worth knowing that several of the bigger islands have their own airports. When visiting Rhodes, I decided to fly directly from London to Rhodes airport, as I was tight on time and there was enough flexibility in my budget to do this. Also, Corfu is a budget-friendly island you are able to fly into.

Ferry: Taking the ferry is the best way to travel between the different islands and from mainland Greece. The cost per ticket varies depending on the distance, but you'll be pleased to know in the off-season some ferries can cost as low as $10. You can book this on sites, such as **Ferryscanner.com**. Of course, with all good things (and budget-friendly things), there is a downside. The weather around the islands can be very windy, which could mean boat delays or motion sickness for passengers. Also, taking the ferry can be the slower option; for example, it can take up to five hours to get to the farthest island from the Athens port.

Buses: Buses are the most budget-friendly way to navigate Corfu. There are two kinds of buses available: the city buses (blue in color) and the intercity buses (green in color), and together these cover the majority of places of interest, so both are a good option. Moreover, buses on Rhodes are straightforward to use and inexpensive, with tickets costing $2–$10 depending on the route. There are public **RODA** buses (blue and white in color); to use these buses you need to purchase a ticket before boarding and validate it on the bus. The other bus company is **KTEL** (orange and white in color), and you can get these tickets from a kiosk in Old Town.

Car rentals: This is my preference for moving around each island, as I love the freedom to be able to follow my own schedule and visit more remote areas. In high season, rentals are around $45 a day and in low season you can snag some bargain rentals for as little as $13 a day. Perfect for if you're visiting with company or want to explore with the new friends you made at your hostel.

Car services: Both **Uber** and **Free Now** operate in Athens and on Thessaloniki. No private drivers/cars are allowed in Greece, so car services use the regular taxi services you can find outside the airport. Expect prices to be slightly cheaper than those found in the United States.

FOOD & DRINK

You can't leave Greece without eating a gyro—scratch that. You can't leave Greece without eating at least three gyros. This is a sandwich made with pita bread, stuffed with either lamb, beef, pork or chicken and topped with lettuce, tomato, onion and tzatziki sauce (cucumber and yogurt). Gyro shops are dotted all around Greece; some good and affordable shops to buy from are **Pitafan** (Rhodes) and **Souvlaki Fres** (Santorini).

For a traditional Greek breakfast, try the bougatsa, a mouthwatering flaky pastry filled with sweet custard or savory cheese. It's very popular to find these at local bakeries, such as **Bougatsa Kanoni** (Corfu), for a low cost. The cheese variety is particularly filling.

When exploring, you will want to keep an eye out for taverna restaurants. Here you can usually enjoy a hearty, filling meal for a reasonable price. Opt for psistaria (grills) or magiremata (cooked dishes) as budget-friendly options.

Greece is known for its fresh produce, so local markets are very much my go-to option for meals when I am exploring the country. **Corfu Central Market** is a great spot if you're touring the island and need a bite. The market offers a wide variety of fresh products, including fruits, vegetables, meat, fish, seafood, dairy, herbs, spices and more. Vendors take pride in offering the best possible products to their customers at affordable prices. You can even find small eateries in the market if you prefer a cooked meal.

Fortunately, many eateries offer a hearty Greek salad as a side dish or starter free of charge. It usually includes fresh produce like tomatoes, cucumbers, olives and feta cheese. This can be used to bulk up any meals to keep you full.

ABOVE
Did you know that Souma Nikolas is the traditional drink of Rhodes? This wine is hard to find off this island, so get it while you can!

THE PERFECT LOW-COST GREEK ISLANDS BUCKET LIST

RHODES

❋ Paddle to **secret beaches on a kayak**. Kayak along the coast on an afternoon adventure. There are so many unique rock formations and hidden caves to explore. Most hostels and hotels mentioned earlier offer affordable kayak rentals or recommendations. **($)**

❋ Dance through the **Valley of Butterflies**. This place is literally something out of a gothic fairy tale, similar to the forest depicted in *Bridge to Terabithia*. The beautiful little waterfalls and wooden bridges will have you feeling like a child on an adventure. If you visit between October and March, the colors in the forest elevate the experience. You will need to pay a small entry fee to enter the nature park. **($)**

❋ Hike to the tranquil **Oasis of Seven Springs**. Another magical place to explore, this activity is perfect for cooling down on a hot day and after a visually gorgeous hike. **(Free)**

- Spot peacocks in **Rodini Park**. Walk in the footsteps of the Romans, in one of the oldest landscaped parks in the world. Discover hidden streams, tranquil ponds and ancient ruins. I have only ever seen peacocks in person a handful of times in real life, but they are beautiful creatures. This is a great place to go peacock spotting. **(Free)**

CORFU

- Stroll the streets of **Corfu Old Town**. Take in the historic highlights, such as **Old Fortress** and **Palace of St. Michael and St. George**, before venturing into secret squares to explore beyond the tourist trail. Fun fact: This is a UNESCO World Heritage site. **(Free)**

- Visit the **Paleokastritsa Monastery**. Paleokastritsa is a small village that is said to be the Greek mythological site of Scheria. This monastery dates back centuries and has a gorgeous must-see interior. **(Free)**

- Hike **Mount Pantokrator** for sweeping panoramic views of the island. This is the highest peak on the island, which of course means it has some of the best views available. If you don't fancy hiking, there is also a drivable road that leads to the summit. **(Free)**

- Have a picnic on **Porto Timoni Beach**. The unique thing about this beach is its double bay formation, essentially creating twin beaches. The beach itself is small and secluded, making it the perfect place for a romantic lunch, a group of friends catching up or a solo traveler looking for some quiet to take in the beauty of nature. The bay offers crystal-clear water for great swimming opportunities.

OPPOSITE
If there is one thing Greece does well, it is breathtaking landscapes.

Amsterdam
NAVIGATING THE CANALS AND COSTS

Amsterdam is the capital of the Netherlands, and one of the most popular tourist destinations in all of Europe. The city is well known for its intricate canal system that weaves through the streets and for the architecture of their iconic narrow houses. One of my first girls' trips as an adult was to Amsterdam, and it was one of my best experiences to date. Very random, but one of the first things I noticed when I arrived was just how tall everyone is.

Some even call the Netherlands the "land of giants," because the average height is much higher than other places in the world. As someone who is 5-foot-9, I felt right at home, like I had met my people! This city has so much to do, including numerous quirky selling points as well as gorgeous scenic streets. Here are a few fun facts about Amsterdam: It has more bikes than people, more canals than Venice and more bridges than Paris.

CITY PROFILE

 Currency, Bank Cards & ATMs: The currency used in Amsterdam and across the Netherlands is the euro (EUR). Mastercard and Visa are the most widely accepted credit cards in the Dutch retail space, and they're accepted at most key establishments, including restaurants, shops and attractions. However, American Express tends only to be accepted by major retailers, although Amex acceptance is growing. It's useful to also carry smaller amounts of euros (cash) for smaller vendors. ATMs are readily available throughout Amsterdam and will allow you to select the language you are most comfortable using. Some ATMs offer a choice between using your "home currency" or "local currency" and you should always opt for local currency, as it tends to have a more favorable exchange rate.

 Climate: Amsterdam experiences mild summers and cool winters. There are distinct seasonal changes, but they aren't super drastic like some other locations in Europe. When I visited around May, it was quite warm; however, being by the water meant there was always a nice breeze, and it was generally lovely to walk around at all times during the day. I recommend spring (April to May) as the best time to visit. It's when the weather begins to start warming up, which means romantic canal strolls and inviting outdoor seating. However, it also means you can avoid the summer rush.

 Safety: Amsterdam is partly known for its Red Light District, wild nightlife and being one of the only countries in Europe with legalized cannabis, which prompts many people to ask, "Well, is it safe to visit?" It will comfort you to know that Amsterdam was ranked the sixth safest major city in the world and number 1 safest in Europe by *The Economist* in 2023. On my first trip to Amsterdam, I traveled with a group of five Black women and on my last trip I visited Amsterdam solo. On both trips I always felt completely safe and never ran in to any trouble. We walked around

at night, including a short visit to a bar in the Red Light District, and again, I never felt unsafe. Would I visit that area at night if I were alone? Probably not, but in general I stay clear of quiet, dimly lit roads when traveling by myself, particularly at night. To conclude, if you stay away from the more questionable parts of Amsterdam, such as the Red Light District, you should have a completely trouble-free trip and enjoy your time.

 Language: The official language of the Netherlands is Dutch, but most residents speak English as a second language.

ABOVE
You've probably seen images of this iconic canal scene, but you need to see it in real life. The calming canals and charming colors are one-of-a-kind in person.

VISITING ON A BUDGET

HOTEL & STAYS

I will start off by saying, at the time of writing this book, accommodation costs in Amsterdam are abnormally high, even for the hostel options. Post-pandemic prices have risen to an unusual rate, which is reflected in my suggestions below.

Low budget: If hostels are your preferred accommodation type, here are a few great suggestions: **Cocomama Hostel ($–$$)** is known for its cozy and welcoming atmosphere. It is right in the city center and close to major attractions, such as the Van Gogh Museum, Anne Frank House and Heineken Experience. Similarly, its sister hotel, **Ecomama ($$)**, is also a great choice if you're more of an environmentally conscious traveler. This hostel is well known for its focus on sustainable and eco-friendly practices and commitment to responsible tourism, not to mention its stylish design. **The Bulldog Hostel ($–$$)** is one of the most famous hostels in Amsterdam. This

may be partly due to it being part of the Bulldog brand, which is popular in Amsterdam's cannabis culture. Other great, affordable options include **Flying Pig Downtown Hostel ($–$$)** and **Stayokay Amsterdam Vondelpark ($–$$)**.

Mid-budget: Moving on to slightly pricier options, let's start with **Hotel Estherea ($$–$$$)**. This charming hotel is in an excellent location along the Singel Canal and has a super artistic interior. Another favorite of mine is **Catalonia Vondel Amsterdam ($–$$)**. This boutique hotel is located close to Vondelpark and is a guest favorite. Other great options include **Backstage Hotel ($$–$$$)**, **The Pavilions**, **The Toren ($$)**, **The Hoxton**, **Lloyd Amsterdam ($$–$$$)** and **Hotel Roemer ($$–$$$)**. These places have excellent locations, are close to many popular sites and some provide an extensive breakfast, so you can potentially save on travel costs and food.

ARRIVED

13 MAY 18

INTERNATIONAL

To highlight, it is easy to get around Amsterdam, so staying in the center of the city isn't a must. Affordable neighborhoods like **Jordaan**, **Zaandam** and **Plantagebuurt** are perfect bases for exploring the city. My favorite is **Zaan Hotel Amsterdam ($$)** in Zaandam.

ABOVE
Did you know Amsterdam is built on 11 million wooden poles?

TRANSPORTATION

Bikes and cycling: Amsterdam is renowned as one of the most bike-friendly cities in the world. Most locals travel by bike in Amsterdam, so there are plenty of bikes around the city. Funnily enough, Amsterdam is one city you're more likely to face bike traffic than car traffic. A refreshing change! You could easily rent a bike for your entire trip for around $10–$15. Renting a bike is not only a very cost-effective way to explore the city, but it also allows you to experience the city as a local. One thing to note is that cyclists have the right-of-way over pedestrians, so be careful. I nearly collided with a bike on more than one occasion. Unlike cars, you don't really hear them coming, so always remain vigilant. One of the most popular bike rentals in Amsterdam is **Mike's Bike Tours**, and some other affordable options are **Frederic Rent a Bike** and **Ajaxbike**.

Public transportation: When I visited Amsterdam, one of the girls in my group was unfortunately unable to ride a bike, which meant biking was not an option for us. However, we were able to make great use of the extensive transportation system around the city. The **OV-chipkaart** is a contactless smart card that you can use on all forms of transport, including trams, buses and Metro lines. If you plan to use public transport multiple times a day, you may want to consider a multiday travel card, which allows unlimited usage throughout its validity. A single one-hour ticket costs around $4.

Ferries: Amsterdam offers free ferry services (except for the Zaanferry) across the IJ River, connecting the city center to various parts of Amsterdam-Nord. Taking the ferry provides a unique perspective of the city and is a budget-friendly way to explore different neighborhoods. I recommend visiting **Buiksloterweg** and **NDSM Wharf**.

FOOD & DRINK

Food markets: Starting off strong with **Foodhallen**, this food hall has so many delicious options that cater to all kinds of diets. It's slightly out of the way of most touristy areas, which means more favorable prices, perfect for budget travelers. My favorite stalls are **Dim Sum Thing** and **Taqueria Lima West**.

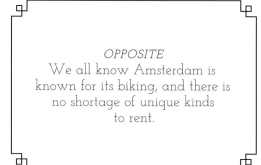

OPPOSITE
We all know Amsterdam is known for its biking, and there is no shortage of unique kinds to rent.

Amsterdam automats: Automats are like vending machine stores where you can pay to get hot food. You can buy burgers and fried foods from these machines, which make the perfect on-the-go meal for only a few dollars. There are 27 **FEBO branches** in Amsterdam alone, so you should have no trouble finding one when you get hungry. While some FEBOs are now equipped with contactless payment panels, most still only accept cash.

Additional cheap-eat suggestions are **Bagels Village**, the perfect spot for delicious bagels and people watching, **Caldi e Freddi** for affordable fresh Italian food, **Maoz Vegan** for very tasty and affordable falafel or **De Hapjeshoek** for a curry sandwich.

The following are slightly pricier snacks, but also must-tries when in Amsterdam: stroopwafels at **van Wonderen**, the famous cookies at **Van Stapele Koekmakerij** and the double-baked fries from either **Fabel Friet, Manneken Pis** or **Vlaams Friteshuis Vleminckx**.

Supermarkets: Amsterdam has a large range of grocery stores with great price points. When I was on my girls' trip to Amsterdam, we cooked most of our meals in our apartment, saving us a good amount, and because there were five of us, we were able to divide grocery costs enough to create very cheap meals. I say "we" cooked, but I hate cooking. So, I let the other ladies cook while I worked out how to run the dishwasher. Consider purchasing groceries from **Dirk, Vomar Voordeelmarkt** or **Lidl**, which offer the cheapest-quality groceries. I must mention, the butter croissants from Lidl are SO GOOD! Most mornings I ate a croissant with ham and cheese and was good for a few hours. This was a lot cheaper to make than purchasing from a café.

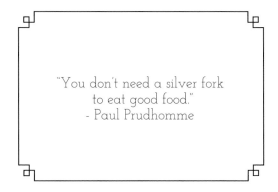

"You don't need a silver fork to eat good food."
- Paul Prudhomme

THE PERFECT LOW-COST AMSTERDAM BUCKET LIST

* The major museums in Amsterdam are pretty pricey, with each costing around **$25** for places like the **Anne Frank Museum** and **Van Gogh Museum**. Having visited both, they were worth forking out the extra money. If you'd like to do the same, here is where the **I amsterdam City Card** could come in handy. Activities included in the card cost are access to 70 museums and attractions around the city, citywide public transport, a canal cruise and bike rental services. In addition, showing your card can get you a discount at some restaurants, theaters and additional activities. Alternatively, the **Amsterdam City Pass** is a slightly cheaper alternative that doesn't include public transport.

* Catch a **free** performance at the **Dutch National Opera & Ballet**. They offer free tickets to lunch concerts on Tuesdays for practice viewing sessions. Lastly, the **Red Light Museum** is extremely insightful. I found it a little sad, but you learn a lot about the industry.

* Have a *Charlie and the Chocolate Factory* experience at **Tony's Chocolonely Super Store**: Here you can make your own chocolate bar. There are loads of flavors to choose from and the whole experience is super fun and unique. **($)**

* Wander around **Noordermarkt**: This is a popular flea market on Sundays and Mondays. **(Free)**

* Take the ferry over to the **A'DAM Lookout** for great views, and if you're not like me and love heights, take a ride on the famous suspended swing. **($–$$)**

* If you're fortunate enough to be visiting during the summer, head to **Vondelpark** for a free open-air cinema show. **(Free)**

* Become a cheese connoisseur: Amsterdam has dozens of cheese stores, which of course offer tons of cheeses and many free samples. Become a cheese connoisseur by visiting a few and ranking the flavors. My suggestion is to start with **Kaashuis Tromp**, which has four branches across the city. **(Free)**

❋ Visit the only floating flower market in the world, **Bloemenmarkt**. The market has existed since 1862. All the flower stalls sit on the houseboats, and it truly is a colorful sight. The market is open all year-round and it's completely free to admire all the flowers. **(Free)**

❋ Explore Amsterdam's **Red Light District** (for educational purposes of course). If you download the **Amsterdam Audio Stories + Map** app and pay a few dollars, you'll have access to over 100 stories told by 22 expert narrators. **De Wallen** area has a fascinating history. The app's self-guided Red Light District tours and adults-only stories are super engaging and worth a listen. **($)**

> "Amsterdam is like the rings of a tree: It gets older as you get closer to the center."
> - John Green

Dublin

CHEAPLY TOURING THE EMERALD ISLE

As the capital of the Republic of Ireland, Dublin has a rich culture, vibrant atmosphere and long, fascinating history. The first time I visited Dublin I was 7 on my first international family holiday ever; I was so excited I didn't even mind where we were going. It was just such a treat to be leaving the country and going to explore. The first thing I remember thinking about the country was just how green it was. Having never left the bustling area of central London, I found it incredibly refreshing to see the rolling green hills and endless green fields. As soon as I returned home, I convinced my parents to put me in Irish dancing classes.

The next time I returned, I was in my 20s. I'm sure it will come as a shock to literally no one that these were very different trips. Funnily enough, it wasn't a country I was desperate to return to, however—cue the power of social media—I randomly came across a video of a young frequent traveler talking about how it was her favorite country in the world out of the 80 countries she had visited. I was astonished, but also very curious. Was there something I had missed? And for anyone who knows how TikTok works, whenever you show even a small inkling of being interested in a topic, you will then be shown videos for months on that same topic. In a nutshell, I gave in and booked a ticket to Dublin. Ladies and gentlemen, I now consider myself to be a convert. From strolling along the iconic River Liffey to experiencing Dublin's legendary pub culture, this chapter will serve as your guide to navigating Dublin on a budget and will highlight all the things that make Dublin so attractive to visitors.

CITY PROFILE

 Currency, Bank Cards & ATMs: The currency used in Dublin is the euro (EUR). Dublin offers a range of convenient payment methods that cater to the needs of modern travelers. Visa and Mastercard, including both debit and credit cards, are widely accepted throughout Ireland; American Express is accepted in some places but not all. Many street markets, smaller cafés and smaller pubs prefer cash payment, so it is always worth having a few emergency euros in your purse or wallet. ATMs are conveniently available to use throughout the city, and you won't have any issues finding one if you are in need.

OPPOSITE
Cities can be just as beautiful in the rain, if not more so! Don't let the weather stop you from taking it all in.

 Climate: Sorry to burst your bubble so early on in this chapter, but no matter what time of year you visit Ireland, you'll likely experience windy and cloudy weather at least once. Also, it isn't uncommon for it to rain in Ireland at any time of year. Of course, I am all about looking at the bright side of things. This means that visiting during the most expensive time of year, summer (June to August), isn't hugely different from visiting in the much more affordable months of September and October. The summer crowds start to thin out and many outdoor festivals and literary events take place. If you plan on beating the summer crowds and hiked prices by visiting in the spring, you may want to rethink your plans. St. Patrick's Day in March is a huge deal and taken very seriously around the entire country. Accommodations fill up quickly, prices are inflated and the entire country basks in merriment. Although this is an epic experience, it's a month to avoid when visiting on a budget. Visiting Dublin on St. Patrick's Day should be a bucket list travel item for later down the line.

Safety: The people of Dublin are known for their friendliness and hospitality, so you have nothing to worry about. Millions of people visit Ireland every year and the majority have a trouble-free trip. Take the usual precautions like watching out for pickpockets and everything should be just fine.

Language: The official language of Ireland is Irish (Gaelic) and English. Although Irish is recognized as the first official language, English is widely spoken and used in most day-to-day conversations. In 2010, the Irish government launched the 20-year strategy for the Irish language, which is designed to strengthen the language in all areas and increase the number of habitual speakers. However, it's pretty unlikely that you will come across anyone in Dublin who doesn't speak a little bit of English. Rest assured, you should have no issues navigating the city.

VISITING ON A BUDGET

HOTEL & STAYS

Low budget: Staying in a shared-room hostel tends to be the most budget-friendly accommodation option when traveling across Europe, and this is the case in Dublin. Some great options are **Jacobs Inn Hostel ($)**, **Kinlay House Hostel ($)** and of course **Generator Dublin ($–$$)**. You may have noticed that the Generator hostel brand has come up a few times throughout this book, and that is because it is an excellent brand for quality hostels. Just something to note for when you're traveling and looking for local hostel options.

Mid-budget: When contemplating what central area to stay in, the **Temple Bar area** emerges as one of the best choices. Some standout hotels here are the **Arlington Hotel O'Connell Bridge ($$)** and **Harding Hotel ($$)**. For a quieter setting, **Castle Hotel ($$$)** is located on the north side and has a charming character. You should also consider staying at **Jurys Inn Dublin Parnell Street ($$)** or **Maldron Hotel Pearse Street ($$–$$$)**. Lastly, **The Clayton Hotel** is slightly farther out of the city, but has great transport links directly to the city center right outside the hotel and offers affordable prices **($$)**.

"Travel makes one modest,
you see what a tiny place you
occupy in the world."
- Gustave Flaubert

TRANSPORTATION

Buses: Dublin boasts an extensive public transport network, making it easy to get around without too much trouble. The Dublin bus system connects all the major attractions and neighborhoods. A single fare ticket typically costs around $3. And here is a **tip:** The buses don't automatically stop at every bus stop, so remember to hail down a bus you'd like to take by putting your arm out. For awareness, buses tend to be late, so be patient when navigating the network. Ireland is a very relaxed country, and visiting from fast-paced London was a real change, so I learned to enjoy the slower pace and lifestyle.

Trams: The **Luas** tram system offers two lines that intersect at several key points and a one-way ticket starts at $2. If you're staying for a few days and intend to use a mixed public transport option, you should look into getting a **Leap Card**, which offers discounted fares on buses, trams and trains.

Biking: Dublin is a bike-friendly city with dedicated cycling lanes and bike-sharing schemes like **Dublinbikes**. If you are confident riding, this is a great budget-friendly option as you can rent a bike for three days for just $6. If you choose this option, you must go through **Phoenix Park** for a scenic ride.

Walking: Dublin has a compact city center, which makes walking a delightful and free way to explore the city.

FOOD & DRINK

Pubs: Pubs are a very popular place for Irish people to mix and drink, so naturally it offers visitors the perfect opportunity to experience Irish social culture. It's very easy to strike up a conversation with a stranger and then feel like you've known them for years. It's nearly impossible to leave an Irish pub having had only one drink, especially with the rounds system. What is the rounds system, you ask? If you're out with Irish people in Ireland, you'll most definitely be offered a drink. One person will go to the bar to order and pay for everyone. This is called "getting a round in," with the unwritten expectation that you will do the same at some point during that drinking session. When on a budget, you should monitor how much you are spending on drinks. Ireland's strong pub culture has a great way of slowly chipping away at your budget if you aren't careful. Some great pub suggestions are **Dame Tavern**, **The Hairy Lemon** and **Mulligan's**. If you're looking for something a little bit more intimate,

ABOVE
Can you really go to Dublin if you don't eat some potatoes at least once? Double points if it's in a pub!

The Brazen Head is a good choice. Eating pub grub can also be an affordable food option as the meals are hearty. **The Celt** has a great bangers and mash (sausage and mashed potatoes), great vibes and good live music. You can expect to pay around **$7–$8** for a pint and **$10–$20** for a complete meal.

Cafés: Cafés are the way to go for an inexpensive hearty breakfast. Think about eating at **Beanhive Café**, known for its friendly staff, delectable pastries and artisanal coffee; or **White Moose Café**, a quirky spot known for its social media presence and creative menu options. On my most recent trip, I popped into **Lemon Jelly** and had a traditional Irish breakfast, which kept me full for five to six hours. Each café mentioned stands out in Dublin's thriving café scene, with meals ranging from **$6–$14**.

Picnicking: Embrace a budget-friendly DIY meal by picking up some local produce from **Moore Street Market** and finding a cute spot in **St. Stephen's Green**.

THE PERFECT LOW-COST DUBLIN BUCKET LIST

* Laugh out loud at a comedy show. One of the best things to do in Dublin is watch a two- to three-hour comedy show at **Chaplin's Comedy Club**. **($)**

* Go on a self-guided street art tour. **Dublinwalls.com** has several street art routes of varying length to explore. See the epic works of Banksy. **(Free)**

* Have a conversation with **Dublin's talking statues**. These are ten statues of Ireland's most influential people at various points around the city. Go on a quest to find them. At each statue, you can scan the QR code and you'll receive a call from the statue telling you about their role in Ireland's history. **(Free)**

* Take a neon life drawing class at **Alternative Dublin**. I've never done anything like it before, and it's such a fun and unique activity. You'll get to use neon paint to draw a living sculpture. The entire room is dark, with only UV light available. Also, you get to create your own souvenir to take home to remember your trip. **($$)**

ABOVE AND OPPOSITE
I love exploring modern
and historic architecture
in any city.

* Snap some photos at **Love Lane**. This was created by artist Anna Doran, and it's super cute. There are cute quotes spread across the wall, and the colors are perfect for a photo background. **(Free)**

* Take to the stage at an **open mic night**. Every Wednesday, Zodiac sessions in **Bruxelles Pub** has an open mic night, and the talent on stage is incredible. If singing is your thing, what a great way to show off your talent, but be sure to register in advance. On the other hand, this is your chance to hear upcoming talent perform before they get blown up and go international. **(Free)**

* If you're visiting Dublin, you must take a quick cheeky dip in the **Forty Foot**; it's pretty much a rite of passage. The Forty Foot is a body of water on the tip of Dublin Bay. It's estimated that people have been swimming in this part of the Irish sea for over 250 years. **(Free)**

Budapest
THE LAND OF ATTAINABLE FAIRY TALES

Budapest is a city I firmly believe is beyond underrated. Whenever I speak to my international friends about places they'd like to visit in Europe, it rarely makes the list. Everyone seems to be sleeping on this absolute European gem. So far, I have visited Budapest twice and I have every intention of returning. On my first trip I was captivated by how much there is to do and how affordable the city is. Having visited both on a girls' trip and solo, I can say this city is perfect for all kinds of travelers.

The city of Budapest, or what I like to call "the land of fairy tales," is one of the most enchanting cities I have ever visited. It has a rich history, vibrant culture and undeniable charm. One thing I love about this city is the juxtaposition between the celebration of an old history with the modern era. On the Buda side you have captivatingly beautiful castles, cobblestone streets, cozy traditional shops, medieval buildings and a quiet ambience. Contrastingly, on the Pest side you have a bustling night life, modern shopping and a lively atmosphere. While each side is distinct, both complement each other perfectly to create a full experience for anyone who visits. This city promises a symphony of experiences without breaking the bank, so in this chapter we're going to focus on discovering Budapest, without scrambling your budget.

CITY PROFILE

 Currency, Bank Cards & ATMs: The official currency of Hungary is the Hungarian forint (HUF). Card payments are widely accepted across the city, especially Visa and Mastercard. The only time I needed to withdraw money on my trips was when I visited Central Market and wanted to buy a fresh fruit juice. Most of the stalls only accept cash and the ATM inside the market has a hefty fee for withdrawal. If this is somewhere you plan to visit to grab some drinks, snacks or souvenirs, I highly recommend preparing some cash in advance. You'd be better off using an ATM owned by a local bank, as they do not charge exorbitant fees for withdrawal.

Climate: Hungary is beautiful all year round, so choosing the best time to visit really depends on your weather preferences and budget. My recommendation is to visit in spring (March to May) when the weather starts to warm up; the city's parks and gardens come to life with blossoms, and the crowds are relatively smaller than in the summertime (June to August). Also, visiting in autumn has many similar benefits. You'll be treated to many wine festivals and cultural events. Lastly, you may want to consider visiting in winter if you are happy to brave the cold. There is nothing more glorious than relaxing in a 104°F (40°C) thermal bath on a freezing winter night. More on the wonder that is thermal baths later in this chapter.

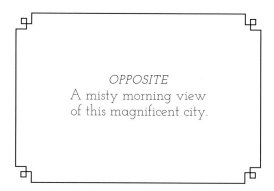

OPPOSITE
A misty morning view
of this magnificent city.

Safety: When my friend and I first decided we were going to go on a last-minute trip to Budapest, I was nervous. I hadn't heard much about Hungary before, and I had my preconceived notions about how I may be treated as a Black woman. Nonetheless, I was amazed by how well I was received. There was no staring or passive aggression and at no point was I made to feel uncomfortable. Budapest isn't renowned for its cultural diversity, and it cannot yet be compared to cities like London and Paris, but as international tourism and expatriate communities increase, attitudes toward people of different ethnic backgrounds have become more open. I personally found locals to be friendly and helpful. Certainly, experiences can differ greatly from person to person, but I highly recommend you approach your visit to Budapest with an open mind. In general, Hungary itself is an extremely safe country to visit. On numerous occasions I walked around by myself at night and in the early hours of the morning, but never had any worries. However, like any big city that attracts tourists, thieves and pickpocketing are common on public transport and other famous spots visited by tourists. As long as you stay vigilant, you should have a completely trouble-free trip.

 Language: The official language spoken in Hungary is Hungarian. As you probably guessed, I do not speak Hungarian, but I managed to navigate everything perfectly fine. Many people in Hungary speak English, so don't be worried! I always have my handy **Google Translate** app downloaded just in case I run in to any barriers, but I never had to use it on either of my trips.

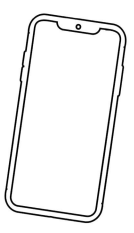

VISITING ON A BUDGET

HOTEL & STAYS

I highly recommend staying on the **Pest side** when visiting and opting to do a day trip to the Buda side to explore. Pest offers a larger selection of accommodations and is more cosmopolitan due to its central location. Also, most of the activities I did on my trip were on the Pest side, so staying there meant less time spent traveling and more time soaking up the city.

BELOW
Even quaint accommodations have no shortage of local art and design!

Low budget: If you're looking for a vibrant hostel with loads of social events and more of a "party" focus, you should consider staying at **Vitae Hostel ($–$$)**. They're known for their social events and are popular with travelers looking to experience Budapest's night life. Alternatively, if like me you prefer accommodation to still be social but much quieter and less party focused, **Maverick Hostel & Ensuites ($)**, **Onefam Budapest ($–$$)**, **Maverick City Lodge ($)** and **Pal's Hostel & Apartments ($–$$)** are great options. These accommodations focus more on community, cultural experiences and opportunities for guests to explore the city.

Mid-budget: On my first trip to Budapest, my friend and I stayed at the **Emerald Hotel & Suites ($$)** downtown. This hotel was super central and just a few steps away from the famous Vaci shopping street. Then, on my second visit I stayed at **Hotel Moments Budapest ($$–$$$)**, located near the Hungarian state opera house. I enjoyed my stay at both these boutique hotels and highly recommend them if your budget is slightly more elastic. Other great options are **Ikonik Parlament ($$)**, **Hotel Rum Budapest ($$)**, **Hotel Palazzo Zichy ($$)** and **Hotel Clark ($$$)**.

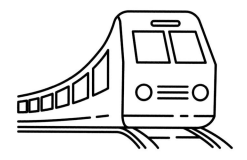

TRANSPORTATION

Getting there: The cheapest and most affordable option for getting from the airport to the city center is taking the **airport bus 100E**. The bus costs around $3, only has three stops (not including the airport) and takes 30 to 45 minutes. It's located a few minutes' walk from the arrivals terminal and is clearly posted. Tickets can be purchased from the BKK customer service center or BKK vending machine at the bus stop.

Cabs: On one of my trips to Budapest, we arrived at around midnight and, due to this being our first time arriving in a new city at night and exhaustion, we wanted to take a cab from the airport to our hotel. Our initial thought was to order a **Bolt**, the most popular car-sharing app in the city. However, it worked out that taking a **yellow taxi** ordered directly from outside the airport was cheaper because of the flat rate.

Trams: Using the tram is by far the best way to get around the city. If you download the **BudapestGO** app, you can get a 24-hour, 72-hour or 7-day travel pass on your phone. Passes offer unlimited rides on public transport, including buses, trams and the Metro. If you plan to use these methods of transport frequently, then the pass is the most cost-effective option. However, if like me you enjoy walking more, you may want to consider purchasing a single ticket. These can be used for a single ride on any of the modes of transport mentioned above. Budapest is a walking-friendly city with many attractions near each other, so you may use one or two single tickets a day.

Biking: Budapest's bike rental service is run through an app called **MOL Bubi**, and it's easy to sign up if this is your preferred method of transport. Prices start from around $2 per day for rentals.

FOOD & DRINK

I would describe the culinary scene in Budapest as super homey. It's the perfect combination of flavors and tradition intertwining to create little unforgettable dining experiences that won't break the bank. Trying at least one traditional dish for me is a must whenever I visit a new country, but I found myself constantly wanting to try different dishes at least once a day. Dishes like goulash and lángos are both dishes I thoroughly enjoyed. Goulash is a hearty Hungarian soup filled with meat and vegetables seasoned with paprika and other spices, and is the perfect meal to keep you full on a colder day (or any day to be honest). Langos is a Hungarian deep-fried flatbread that can be topped with either sweet or savory toppings. It is perfect for any meal, particularly breakfast. Not to forget the delicious pastry that is chimney cake, a sweet, spiral-shaped pastry coated in cinnamon and sugar.

Retró Lángos is a very popular spot for eating lángos, and after visiting I could completely see why. They offer both savory and sweet options, prompt service, friendly staff and affordable prices. One of them was enough to fill me up for a few hours. An alternative option is **Lángos Land**. Furthermore, there are numerous stalls in the **Central Market Hall** that sell authentic goulash.

Ruins bars are a must when in Budapest; even if you don't drink, you'll still be able to enjoy an affordable menu. These are bars that are in former abandoned buildings, which gives them a super unique vibe. They are an integral part of Budapest's night life. My preferred drink in Budapest is always tokaji, a sweet wine that is scrumptious. It's often referred to as "the wine of kings" due to its historical significance and quality. I highly recommend a trip to **Szimpla Kert** ruins bar.

If you are in more of a rush and just want a quick bite to keep you going for a couple of hours, bakeries are the way to go for large, filling pastries that will only set you back a few dollars! Some delicious bakery options are **Művéesz Kávéház Café**, **Pékmühely**, **Zsuzsi's Cuki Desserts** and **Fröhlich Bakery**. My favorite is Pékmühely, which has the most delicious, large cinnamon rolls.

ABOVE
I tasted some of the freshest pressed juice at the Central Market Hall!

As mentioned earlier in this chapter, the city has many vibrant markets that offer fresh local produce, such as fruits, breads, cheeses and meats. The **Great Market Hall** is the best location to explore this food option. Portions tend to be large for the prices you'll pay, and there is a huge variety of both cold and hot choices.

ABOVE
Did you know Szimpla Kert was rated the third best bar in the world?

THE PERFECT LOW-COST BUDAPEST BUCKET LIST

✳ Budapest is world renowned for its **thermal baths**. Fun fact, I actually found this out when I visited the Hungary pavilion at Expo 2020. I must say, they had one of the best pavilions at the exhibition. I digress, but long story short, you can't come to Budapest without visiting one. Some of the more popular baths, such as **Gellért Thermal Bath ($$)** and **Széchenyi Thermal Bath ($$)**, can be quite pricey. Consider getting a three-hour **Fast Track ticket**, which is usually available for morning and afternoon slots. This is a more affordable option to the full-day ticket. In all honesty, we purchased the full-day ticket before I knew about this, and we only spent around two hours at the thermal bath. Don't forget to bring your own flip-flops, or you'll have to purchase some. A more affordable alternative is visiting one of the more local baths like **Palatinus Baths**, which currently costs around **$7**. **Mandala Day Spa** is another option. **($–$$)**

OPPOSITE
Budapest's thermal baths: where relaxation meets history.

❋ Watch a performance at the **Royal Opera House**. You can grab balcony seats for as low as **$2** to an epic performance and they have affordable wine inside. Similarly, tickets to **Budapest Jazz Club** start from around **$5**. **($)**

❋ Catch the sunrise at **Fisherman's Bastion**. The castle is one of the most beautiful structures in the city and is a must-visit site. The best viewpoint can be taken in from the upper balconies. This area usually has a small fee, but if you go first thing in the morning for the sunrise the barriers will be open. The charge only applies from 9 a.m. each day. **(Free)**

❋ Wander through the **Palvolgyi Caves**. When you enter the cave, you will be treated to some stunning rock formations. This is a great activity if you're feeling adventurous and want to explore the city from a deeper perspective. **($)**

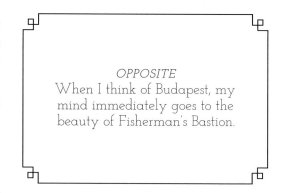

OPPOSITE
When I think of Budapest, my mind immediately goes to the beauty of Fisherman's Bastion.

❋ Ride on the **Zugliget Chairlift**. If you aren't scared of heights, this is a unique activity not many visitors do. This two-person chairlift will give you gorgeous forest views and a panoramic visual of the city. **($)**

❋ Want a unique, lighthearted experience? Visit the **Flippermúzeum Pinball Museum**. This museum houses Europe's largest pinball collection; you can even play the first pinball machine ever made, and they have loads of original arcade games. There are six or seven rooms full of games, so plenty to occupy yourself with. **($)**

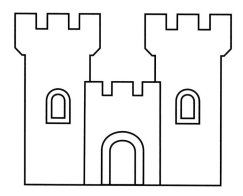

Lisbon
THE AFFORDABLE HIDDEN GEM OF EUROPE

The sun-drenched city of Lisbon has remained under the radar for years, but not anymore! I'm sure Lisbon needs no introduction today, as everyone is finally waking up to this vibrant, colorful city with its picturesque neighborhoods, delicious pastries, cobblestone streets and mosaic-adorned sidewalks. Brace yourself, because when you visit the "City of Seven Hills" you may never want to leave—it's that easy to fall in love with Lisbon. I first visited on a whim, a last-minute trip booked two days before I was set to depart. Preparing for the trip was slightly chaotic and I ended up spending more money than necessary because of poor planning and lack of due diligence. However, I have learned all those lessons so you can avoid my mistakes.

CITY PROFILE

 Currency, Bank Cards & ATMs: The official currency of Portugal is the euro (EUR). Mastercard and Visa are widely accepted in hotels, restaurants, shops and tourist attractions. However, I recommend carrying some petty cash in euros for market purchases. ATMs are widely available across the city at most banks and shopping centers.

 Climate: Lisbon enjoys a Mediterranean climate, which consists of warm, dry summers and rainy, mild winters. Spring is considered one of the best times to visit, as the weather begins to get warmer and outside activities begin to resume. However, my preference has always been to visit in the early autumn (September to October), as the weather is still hot, prices are lower than the peak summer months, there are fewer crowds and more festivals and events take place.

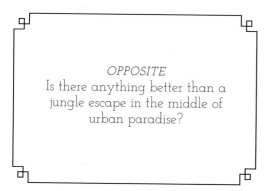

OPPOSITE
Is there anything better than a jungle escape in the middle of urban paradise?

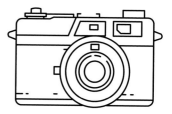

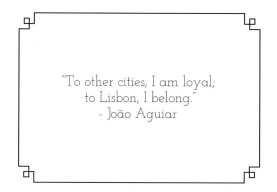

"To other cities, I am loyal;
to Lisbon, I belong."
- João Aguiar

Safety: Portugal is a safe country to visit solo, with friends or with a partner. It's been ranked one of the safest countries in the world, and this was truly reflected in my experiences in the country and in Lisbon. Crime rates are low in the city, so you have nothing to worry about. There is a large expat community in Lisbon from a diverse range of backgrounds, so visiting as a Black woman was not an issue.

Language: The official language of Portugal is Portuguese. English is widely spoken in Lisbon and many of the surrounding towns, such as Sintra, Cascais and Costa da Caparica. English is essentially a second language in Portugal, so you will have no trouble getting around and communicating with people when you need to.

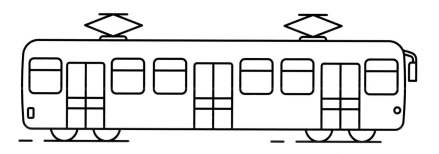

VISITING ON A BUDGET

HOTEL & STAYS

Short-term homestays: Most of the times I have visited Lisbon, I have opted to stay in either an Airbnb or a VRBO apartment. This is mostly because I often book late, and these tend to be the most affordable options for last-minute bookings. One of the best things to do when exploring Lisbon is to stay in the heart of the city. I'd recommend searching for properties in the **Bairro Alto ($$)**, **Baixa ($$)** or **Chiado ($$)** areas.

Low budget: Lisbon welcomes budget travelers with a great range of quality hostels. My favorite is **Yes! Lisbon Hostel ($–$$)** because of the great location, smack in the city center and close to popular tourist sites, but you should also consider **Lisboa Central Hostel ($)**, a cozy hostel that provides a welcoming atmosphere and is known for its social aspects; **Lisbon Destination Hostel ($–$$)**, which is located in the popular Bairro Alto district, making it the ideal place to stay for younger travelers looking to immerse themselves in Lisbon's night life; **Good-morning Solo Traveller Hostel ($–$$)**, a charming hostel situated in the historic Alfama district that has a strong focus on solo travelers and

helping them navigate the city; or **Sunset Destination Hostel ($–$$)**, the perfect place to stay for its Instagram-worthy scenic view. The hostel is perched on a hill overlooking Lisbon's iconic landscape.

Low to mid-budget: On my last visit to Lisbon, I booked everything super last minute and many of my favorite places to stay that are closer to the city center were actually sold out, which meant I had to stay farther out. I stayed at **EXE Liberdade ($$)** and to my surprise I thoroughly enjoyed the hotel and location. The location was close to great transport links, the staff were awesome (even gave us a late check-out for free, because our flight was in the evening) and the facilities were super clean.

Mid-budget: If hotels are more your pace, then here are some great options for you to consider: **Portugal Boutique City Hotel ($$-$$$)** is a boutique hotel, located in the heart of Lisbon's historic center, and is inspired by Portuguese decor. The hotel's proximity to key attractions is a big selling point. **My Story Hotel Rossio ($$–$$$)**, **Hotel Lisboa Plaza ($$$)**, **1908 Lisboa Hotel ($$–$$$)** and **Hotel Mundial ($$–$$$)** also have great offers that are comfortable and highly recommended.

TRANSPORTATION

Walking: I personally found this the best way to get around Lisbon, besides, I needed a way to burn off the calories from all the pastries I was enjoying. Walking around the town on sunny days was such a refreshing experience, and I felt like it was the best way to take in everything. Be aware that the "City of Seven Hills" is just that: very hilly! You'll be met with steeply inclined hills and cobbled mosaic streets and be essentially hiking a lot, so make sure you bring comfortable shoes with a good grip. I slipped more than once in my Converse sneakers.

Public transportation: Aside from walking, public transport is the next best affordable option for budget travelers planning to move around the city. Lisbon has a sophisticated public transport system comprised of the Metro, trams and buses. The **commuter train** operated by CP is the best option to visit farther attractions such as Sintra and Cascais for a day trip. Lisbon has six tram lines, and while these are all a functional and efficient mode of transport, they're also an iconic and fun way to explore the city. The Tram 12 line goes through many popular neighborhoods and attractions. Lastly, taking the bus is a good option to access areas not covered by the tram or Metro.

ABOVE
Did you know the idea for trams in Lisbon came from the United States?

ABOVE
Did you know the pastels de
nata at Lisbon's Pastéis de Belém
are so revered that the centuries-
old secret recipe has never been
written down?

Uber/Bolt: Ride-share services do not cost as much in Lisbon as in other major cities around Europe. We used this service specifically at night or when we were running late. The cost divided between my friend and me was similar to what we would have spent on public transport for the day.

FOOD & DRINK

Eating pastel de nata is necessary when visiting Lisbon. This super delicious egg custard tart is one of my favorite dessert snacks. Everyone says that **Pastéis de Belém** serves the best ones, but I strongly disagree. The ones made at **Manteigaria Bakery** are the clear winners of the pastel de nata war, in my humble opinion. Make sure you try both, so you can make a fair judgment for yourself.

My favorite breakfast spot has to be **The Folks ($5–$12)**, where I ate the mango rice porridge on most days, and it was so delicious. The flavors were rich and I felt full for the next few hours of activities.

A few other delicious low-cost eateries are **Quiosque de São Paulo** for Portuguese snacks **($5–$12)**, **Madam Bo ($5–$12)** for delicious dumplings, **The Pizza Wizard ($5–$12)** for affordable pizza slices and **Tu & Eu Bistro ($10–$25)**. One of my favorite foods is Mexican tacos, and **La Malquerida** sells delicious tacos for a euro each between 6 p.m. and 7 p.m. every day.

THE PERFECT LOW-COST LISBON BUCKET LIST

* Rank the *miradouros* dotted around the **Alfama district**. *Miradouros* means "viewpoint" in Portuguese. Remember when I mentioned that Lisbon is the city of seven hills? Well, that means it is home to some of the best views you'll see in Europe. Spend an afternoon ranking your favorites. **(Free)**

* Enjoy a **Fado performance** at **Tasca do Chico**, where there is a live performance every day at 8 p.m. There is no entry fee, but you will have to buy something (anything) on the menu. **($)**

* Ride **Tram 28** from beginning to end. Instead of paying for the pricey hop-on bus, you can hop on Tram 28 to see all the best sights in the city. The yellow tram is an iconic feature of Lisbon and riding one should be on your bucket list. You can purchase a ticket from the conductor directly on board. **($)**

* Climb the **Santa Justa Elevator** without the price tag. Enjoy some of the best views of the city without paying to go up the Santa Justa Elevator. Walk along the path behind the Carmo Convent, along Travessa Dom Pedro de Menezes. Climb up a few steps and you'll see a bridge connected to the Santa Justa Elevator. Once you cross it, you'll see the exact same views over Lisbon. **(Free)**

* Walk down **Rua De Silva (Green Street)**. This charming alleyway is an idyllic botanical paradise tucked away behind the main streets. The walkway is lined with plants, old buildings and unique shops, perfect for grabbing a coffee or shopping for unique souvenirs. **(Free)**

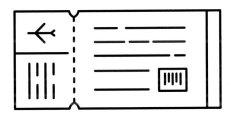

❋ Chill with locals at **Docas de Santo Amaro Docks**, where you'll find a small number of bars and restaurants. Grab a cocktail and take a seat under the bridge for sunset. **($)**

❋ Check out the graffiti in **Panorâmico de Monsanto**. This abandoned building is filled with graffiti art and has some of the best views in the city. **(Free)**

❋ Snap a picture with the iconic **Elevador da Bica**. This funicular railway line is the best place to snap a photo with the iconic tram cart without having the stress of trying to catch it at a bus stop. In the morning, you will find a stationary cart, perfect for getting all your shots. **(Free)**

> "You either love or hate Lisbon, but it never leaves you indifferent."
> - Raul Brandão

Croatia

SUN-KISSED TRANQUILITY WITHOUT OVERSPENDING

Last, but most definitely not least, I will be giving you the rundown on the beautiful country that is Croatia. Croatia is home to stunning lakes, luscious forests and breathtaking coastlines that are a must-see when visiting Europe. Whether you're visiting to relax on a pristine beach or to discover the history of their medieval cities, you'll thoroughly enjoy your visit. My first trip to Croatia was a last-minute sister trip we randomly planned a few days before. I didn't know what to expect, as I hadn't known many people who had traveled to the country before. One thing that really stuck out to me was how charming Split was. My favorite cities are the ones that offer a modern twist on older landscapes, and the city did this so well.

Croatia is a country I could return to again and again; I find that there is always so much to do, see and experience. Unfortunately, prices to visit have been steadily increasing yearly as more travelers discover the hidden gems of the country, but it is still much more affordable than many of its European counterparts. Now, let's unveil the tips to navigating frugal travel around Croatia's diverse destinations.

CITY PROFILE

 Currency, Bank Cards & ATMs: The currency used in Croatia is the euro. Fun fact: Croatia only adopted the euro on January 1, 2023, when it became the 20th country member of the euro area. Up until then, the currency used was the Croatian kuna. ATMs are widely available, so you shouldn't have a problem finding one if you need. Again, using official banks means preferable exchange rates, so look out for ATMs at **OTP Bank**, **Zagrebačka Banka or Addiko Bank AG**. Visa, Mastercard and American Express are widely accepted across the country, but some popular bars and remote beach restaurants will only accept cash, so make sure you have some euros handy.

Climate: If you're on a budget, the best month to visit Croatia is late September to October. It's the beginning of off-season, so things like accommodation and flights reduce greatly in price. Every time I have visited Croatia, it has been in September. The weather was warm, there weren't huge crowds, many activities had offers and our hotels were a fraction of the price.

 Safety: Croatia is one of the safest countries in Europe, and this was reflected in my experiences when I visited the country. The crime rate in Croatia is low, and I felt safe walking around at night.

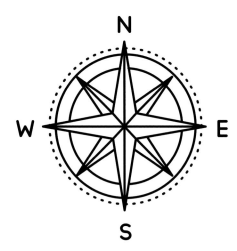

 Language: The official language spoken in Croatia is Croatian, but you can navigate fine without speaking the language. Many people, particularly in the tourist hot spots, speak English and you'll find that signs, menus and important information are often available in English. As always, I do recommend you learn a few basic phrases, as this can enhance your travel experience, allowing you to connect more with locals in smaller towns.

ABOVE
A lovely warm day
in September, free of
large crowds.

VISITING ON A BUDGET

HOTEL & STAYS

Split

Low budget: Hostel Dvor ($–$$) is a smaller hostel with modern facilities and 13 charming rooms with access to both the beach and the city center. For an option even closer to the city center, consider staying at **Hostel Spinut**. **($)**

Mid-budget: The midrange hotels in Split offer a great blend of affordable and comfortable options. The Old Town area of Split is ideal for budget travelers. The boutique **Heritage Hotel Cardo ($$–$$$)** is nestled within the walls of the popular Diocletian's Palace. There is nothing more bougie on a budget than enjoying the luxury of a historical palace without the high price tag. Furthermore, **Palace Suites Heritage Hotel ($$)** offers a similar enchanting stay. For a more tranquil stay closer to the water, **Hotel Villa Diana ($$)** and **Hotel Luxe ($$)** are great options. Lastly, for those looking to cook their own meals, **Divota Apartment Hotel ($$–$$$)** offers apartment-style accommodation with access to kitchenettes.

Dubrovnik

Low budget: Dubrovnik Old Town Hostel ($–$$) is a prime budget option for staying in Dubrovnik, and it's even located within the ancient city walls, so you'll be experiencing an authentic stay while spending an affordable amount. Other great options include **Hostel Villa Angelina Old Town ($–$$)**, an affordable hostel nestled into the city walls of Dubrovnik's Old Town. Its prime location allows travelers to fully immerse themselves in the city's historical ambience. **Hostel Sol ($)** is a short walk from the city's historical center. A great thing about this hostel is it has its own kitchen, so you'll be able to prepare your meals to save those extra coins. Also, **Hostel Villa Garden ($–$$)** is slightly farther out from the city center, but still a short trip to all the main attractions. This family-run hostel offers an intimate feel and welcoming atmosphere for travelers seeking a more personal touch.

Low to mid-budget: On one of my trips to the city I was seeking a more spacious accommodation and I stayed in a privately owned apartment I found on **Booking.com**. It was located a short 15-minute commute to the city center, was super spacious, had a kitchen to prepare meals and the host was great and very helpful with recommendations.

Apartments: A trick I sometimes use if I am on a tighter budget is contacting apartment hosts and owners directly. I usually find the providers on accommodation booking sites, then find the owner's personal details on their own websites or social media and try my luck at a discounted rate. This tends to be beneficial to both parties as it removes the commission taken by third-party platforms like Airbnb.

Mid-budget: When contemplating where to stay, here are some great options you should consider: **Hotel Lapad ($$)** is located in the charming Lapad Bay area for those seeking a tranquil retreat away from the bustling center of Old Town, but still remains connected to main attractions. The nearby promenade is lined with affordable restaurants and cafés, which is handy for organizing meals. Another great option is **Hotel Petka ($$)**, whose interior design is inspired by its picturesque Gruz harbor location and offers great views of the Adriatic Sea. **Hotel Lero ($$–$$$)** is slightly on the higher end of these suggestions, but they do a great job of providing a luxury experience for an affordable price tag. My favorite thing about this option is the extensive breakfast buffet available. Lastly, **Hotel Komodor ($$)** provides comfortable, clean rooms perfect for any visit.

ABOVE
The hostel I stayed at felt like a mini apartment! So clean and cozy and homey.

TRANSPORTATION

Getting there: When planning a trip to Croatia on a budget, it's important to play around with which airport you're going to fly into, whether that is Split Airport or Dubrovnik Airport. There are many great long-distance bus options, such as **Arriva Bus**, **Croatia Bus** and **Čazmatrans** to transport you to your destination.

Buses: When it comes to getting around on a budget, city buses are good value for the money. The network is extensive, buses run frequently and it's a reliable mode of transport. The main local operators are **Libertas** in Dubrovnik and **Promet Split** in the Split area. **GetByBus** is a great tool for mapping bus routes, and you can book your tickets through the website.

Car rentals: When I visited Croatia with my sister, we decided to rent a car, because it was the fastest way to get around with the limited time we had, and the rental prices were affordable for us during the off-season. A car is particularly useful if you'd like to visit popular sites such as Plitvice Lakes and Krka National Park. In addition, renting a car may be a cheaper option than taking the bus if there are two or more of you traveling together. We used **Rentalcars.com** to book a car for pickup directly from the airport. **Tip:** If you are traveling during the off-season, you may be able to snap up a better rental car rate by negotiating in person with various companies when you arrive at the airport. I have managed to secure a 10 to 20 percent discount off the website prices with this method.

Car shares: Croatia is an incredible country for road trips. If you're more of an adventurous spirit, you may want to consider using **Blablacar.com** to source a carpool option. While I have not personally used this method, I know a number of people who have and enjoyed the experience. This option is also popular with locals.

Rent a boat: This can be a pricey option, but hear me out. If you're on a group trip, this is a must if you're staying in a coastal city. Renting a boat is much more affordable in a large group, as the cost is split among several people. There are over 1,200 small islands off the coast just waiting for you to explore them. Many small islands make their own honey, wine and olive oil, so you are in for these culinary treats. If you're traveling solo, there are public ferries available to visit some of the islands. I recommend visiting Lopud. Also, this is the perfect way to do a freestyle "yacht week."

FOOD & DRINK

Many restaurants offer what is known as *marenda*. *Marenda* is a Croatian tradition that offers a brunch-type meal for a lower cost than regular dining.

Visiting a coastal town means fresh seafood being offered daily by many restaurants. However, be careful, as many establishments sell seafood by the kilo, so you may not be aware of the exact costs of your meal until the bill arrives.

OPPOSITE
One of the many unbelievable caves that dot the Croatian shore.

Like many countries in Europe, local bakeries are a purse saver in Croatia. You'll not want to miss trying a burek. This is a phyllo pastry pie with meat that is so delicious. This thick, filled pastry usually costs only a few dollars and is the perfect treat to eat for a filling breakfast.

Pazar Market in Split is the perfect place to pick up some fresh produce to nibble on for lunch. The homemade cheeses, olives, breads and honey have budget-friendly prices, which is ideal for a makeshift lunch on the go.

Many restaurants offer a platter option, and the prices are slightly higher **($10–$25)**, but meals can easily be shared between two or three people, so they can be well priced if you have a slightly wider budget. One of my favorite spots in Dubrovnik that offers this is the popular **Lady Pi-Pi** terraced restaurant. The meat platter is a great choice for a super filling lunch, and the restaurant has great service and views.

Tip: If you're stuck for choice on where to eat, utilize the "cheap eats" filter on **Google Maps** or **Trip Advisor®**.

ABOVE
Croatian food shocked me
pleasantly in so many ways.

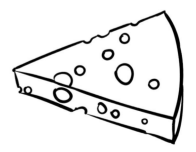

THE PERFECT LOW-COST CROATIA BUCKET LIST

SPLIT

❋ Spot *Game of Thrones* filming locations in **Diocletian's Palace**. Sharpen your swords (theoretically, of course) and explore Split on a themed walking tour to learn the fascinating history about these locations. **GetYourGuide** offers a number of affordable options. **($$)**

❋ **Plitvice Lakes National Park** and **Krka National Park** are breathtakingly gorgeous national parks around one hour outside of Split. In my opinion, these are must-see places. They do run slightly higher prices, costing around **$42**. However, if you're fortunate enough to be visiting in September or October, you can snag a ticket for around **$21**. **($$)**

❋ Climb the steps to **Marjan Park**. This is a great way not only to see epic views of the city, but also to enjoy a picnic lunch after a scenic hike. **(Free)**

❋ Spend the day **beach hopping**. There are a ton of amazing public beaches across Croatia, so it's only right you spend a day lounging in the sun, enjoying the crystal-clear blue sea. One of the best beaches is **Mljet Island**. It's almost always deserted and it's a beautiful beach. **(Free)**

DUBROVNIK

❋ Walk the **Old City wall**. Now, this isn't necessarily a hidden gem as it's probably the most popular thing to do in Dubrovnik. However, I rarely find that people mention the cost of this activity when talking about their experience. The entrance fee alone is close to **$40**, but you won't be paying that if you buy the **Dubrovnik Pass** for **$40**. Not only will you get access to the Old City wall, but you'll also be able to access many other popular places, such as **Rector's Palace**, **Minčeta Tower** and **Fort Bokar**, as well as the city museums and a bus pass.

❋ Go **cliff diving**. Cliff diving is one of the most exhilarating things you can do. I've done it four times now and every time it has been so much fun. **Buža Bar** is a cliffside bar with access through a discreet "hole in the wall" entrance that is a popular spot for cliff diving. **(Free)**

ABOVE AND OPPOSITE
Exploring the Old City wall has to be one of my favorite activities in Dubrovnik. Just look at these views!

PASSPORT PRIVILEGE AND RESPONSIBLE TRAVEL

As the world continues to be increasingly connected, travel has become more accessible than ever before. People can embark on life-changing journeys across the globe that allow them to experience new cultures, foods, environments and ways of life and create memories to last a lifetime. However, as the travel industry develops and continues to flourish, some critical issues come to light: the concepts of passport privilege and responsible travel.

"Passport privilege" refers to the advantages that individuals from certain countries have when it comes to international travel. It usually means there are fewer barriers to being granted access to different destinations. An example would be having visa-free or visa-on-arrival options for multiple countries. I am very thankful for the privileges having a British passport has afforded me over the years. It has meant that I don't often have to worry about choosing where to travel or costly visa fees.

This disparity creates a stark contrast in the experiences of travelers from different countries. I often find that speaking about passport privilege makes people feel uncomfortable, but it's important to acknowledge it if you wish to be a more mindful traveler.

The ability to travel for leisure is a privilege and with this comes a responsibility to create a positive impact on the communities we visit. As an influencer, content creator and frequent traveler, I take my platform very seriously. My job is not only to inspire my followers with stories of my fun adventures and stunning backdrops, but to foster deeper thought about the impact I have on the world and how I can leave each place I travel to having made a positive impact. As lovers of travel, we must be intentional in considering the implications of our journeys, particularly in terms of social, economic and environmental aspects. With this in mind, here are some ways travelers can become more mindful about how they navigate the world.

SOCIAL CONSIDERATIONS

* **Respect rules:** We have all heard the stories of badly behaved travelers who don't follow the clearly signed rules. The latest story I heard was about a lady who climbed into the Trevi Fountain to fill up her water bottle. Yikes! Signs have been posted for a reason, and they often have to do with the preservation of a site.

* **Embrace the local culture:** One of the best things about traveling is learning about the local culture and customs. Take the time to learn a little bit of the local language.

* **Eat locally:** Food is so much more than nourishment; it offers a valuable insight into the traditions of a region. Try local cuisines and specialty dishes.

ECONOMIC IMPACTS

* **Support local businesses:** When it comes to spending money abroad, choosing where to purchase from can have a massive impact on the local community. By having dinner in a small family-owned restaurant, going on a local-led walking tour and buying food from local markets, you are helping inject money directly into the local economy. You're also helping someone create a better life for themselves and their family.

* **Travel off-season:** Planning a trip during low season means that you can support local communities when they need it most.

ENVIRONMENTAL STEWARDSHIP

* **Avoid flying if possible:** Flying is one of the main factors responsible for global warming. Consider taking alternative methods of transport when it is available, such as trains and buses. In addition, reducing layovers and country coupling can reduce the number of flights you're taking. Country coupling is when travelers combine visits to multiple countries in shorter journeys to minimize time spent traveling and to take fewer flights overall.

* **Minimize your waste:** Carrying around a refillable water bottle and saying no to receiving plastic bags in shops are great ways to reduce your personal waste.

* **Offset your carbon footprint:** There are a number of ways travelers can offset their carbon emissions. One of my favorites is the **One Tree Planted** website. The site allows you to calculate your total carbon emissions and pay a monthly fee, whereby the organization will plant trees on your behalf (where they are most needed in the world) to offset your carbon footprint.

Lastly, educate others on being responsible travelers. Many people are unaware of the implications their actions have when they are abroad. Start discussions around responsible travel with your friends and family.

INTO THE WORLD
YOU GO

And that's a wrap! I hope that all the information in this book has you excited and ready to take on the adventure of traveling to Europe on a budget. As you embark on this amazing journey, remember budget travel is about prioritizing experiences and focusing on creating epic memories through interactions with locals, seeing breathtaking views, eating new cuisines and trying new activities. So, go on then, the world is waiting for you.

ALBANIA

AMSTERDAM

ARRIVAL
22 FEB 18
INTERNATIONAL

MALDIVES

IMMIGRATION
ARRIVAL
← 24 JUL 17 →
INTERNATIONAL

RHODES

PERU

AUSTRIA

LAKE COMO

JORDAN

BUDAPEST

ACKNOWLEDGMENTS

First, I'd like to thank God, without whom I would be nothing. I'd like to thank my mum and two sisters (Loretta and Omolola), as well as my close friends. It isn't an easy feat having a family member or friend who travels as frequently as I have over the last ten years, but you've all surrounded me with nothing but encouragement, love and prayers. I'm in awe of how amazing you all are. You've all shown such understanding when I've needed to miss special events for work trips or I'm not always available to meet up. I hope I am able to continue to make you all proud.

Thank you to my brilliant editor, Franny Donington, for asking me to write this book and in doing so recognizing that we need a diverse range of voices in the travel sphere and wider publishing world as well as for all her helpful suggestions and hard work on ensuring this book was a great read. Furthermore, to Elena Van Horn, who was able to embody my entire personality through the design of each page. And to the entire team at Page Street Publishing for making this book a reality.

I'd like to thank myself, for having the self-belief that I could write an entire book using my knowledge from travel, for having the bravery to travel globally even when it wasn't the norm for a person of my ethnicity or socio-economic background, and for chasing after my dreams through massive uncertainties. It took me years to build the self-confidence to post online and look at where it has gotten me!

Furthermore, I'd like to thank my followers and everyone in my online community for virtually following me on all my trips, leaving comments, messaging me recommendations, checking in on me when I've been quiet in posting and all-round just being amazing people.

Lastly, I'd like to thank anyone who bought this book. I sincerely hope you can embark on adventures beyond your wildest imagination and enjoy everything this world has to offer.

ABOUT THE AUTHOR

Tonia Hope is a 20-something-year-old, multiple award-nominated travel content creator and blogger from London, England. It's her passion to inspire her online community by creating lively content to share her epic travel adventures. Tonia shares stories that evoke a strong sense of wanderlust, enticing her followers to swiftly book their next getaway. As a mid-budget, plus-size Black traveler, Tonia aims to make the travel space more diverse through visibility, education and insights into her travel experiences. As someone who has traveled on various budgets across the years, she has gained an excess of knowledge. Tonia loves exploring Europe every summer and frequents countries such as France, Italy, Hungary and Spain.

FOLLOW TONIA ON

※ **Instagram:** @ToniaHope_

※ **Tiktok:** @ToniaHope

※ **Youtube:** @ToniaHope

※ **Website:** toniahope.com

INDEX